RULERS OF INDIA

Aurangzib

RULERS OF INDIA

Aurangzib

AND THE DECAY OF THE MUGHAL EMPIRE

STANLEY LANE - POOLE, B.A.

GYAN

Published by

GYAN

Gyan Publishing House
5, Ansari Road
Daryaganj, New Delhi-110002
Phone: 011-47034999, 9811692060
E-mail: books@gyanbooks.com

Distribution Network
gyanbooks.com
India, USA, Canada, UK, Australia, France

ISBN: 978-81-212-8977-1 (PB)
First Published, 1896

2nd Impression 2023

Printed at: Gyan Press, Delhi.

RULERS OF INDIA AURANGZIB

AUTHOR: STANLEY LANE - POOLE

Rulers of India

EDITED BY

SIR WILLIAM WILSON HUNTER, K.C.S.I., C.I.E.

M.A. (OXFORD): LL.D. (CAMBRIDGE)

AURANGZÍB

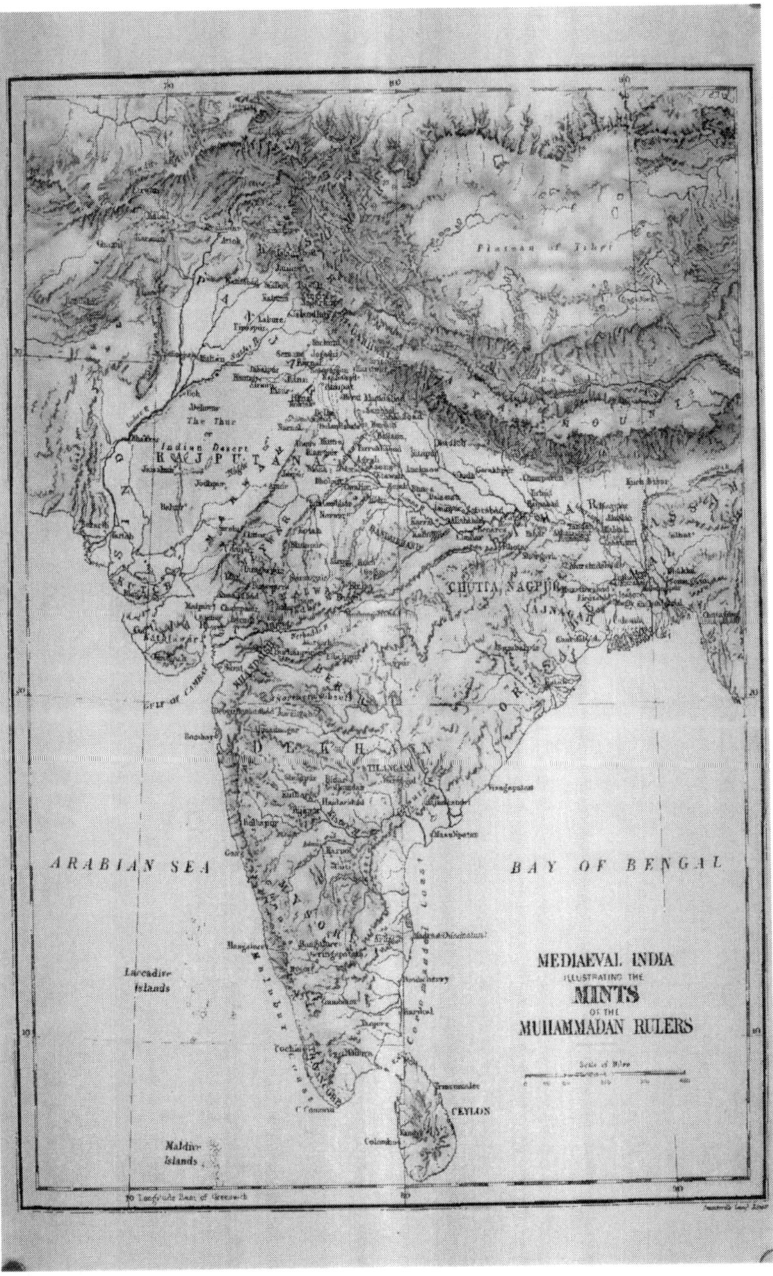
MEDIAEVAL INDIA
ILLUSTRATING THE
MINTS
OF THE
MUHAMMADAN RULERS
ARABIAN SEA
BAY OF BENGAL
Plateau of Tibet
RAJPUTANA
CHUTIA NAGPUR
DEKHAN
TILANGANA
Laccadive Islands
Maldive Islands
CEYLON
Scale of Miles

AURANGZÎB

RULERS OF INDIA

Aurangzib

AND THE DECAY OF THE MUGHAL EMPIRE

By STANLEY LANE-POOLE, B.A.

AUTHOR OF THE CATALOGUE OF ORIENTAL AND INDIAN COINS IN THE BRITISH MUSEUM
THE LIFE OF VISCT. STRATFORD DE REDCLIFFE, ETC.

THIRD THOUSAND

Oxford

AT THE CLARENDON PRESS: 1896

NOTE ON AUTHORITIES

The most important contemporary European authority for the early part of Aurangzíb's reign is the French physician Bernier, who lived in India from 1659 to 1666, and whose *Travels* have recently been admirably edited by Mr. Constable. Bernier writes as a philosopher and man of the world: his contemporary Tavernier (1640–1667) views India with the professional eye of a jeweller; nevertheless his *Travels*, of which Dr. Ball has produced a scientific edition, contain many valuable pictures of Mughal life and character. Dr. Fryer's *New Account of India* is chiefly useful as a description of the Maráthá power under Sivají, for the author during his visit to India (1672-81) did not extend his travels further north than Súrat. Like Fryer, Ovington (1689–92) did not go to the Mughal Court, and his *Voyage to Suratt* contains little beyond what the English merchants of Bombay and Súrat (the only places he visited) chose to tell him. Something may be gleaned from Yule's elaborate edition of Hedges' *Diary* as to the Mughal provincial administration in 1682–4; and Dr. Gemelli Careri's visit to Aurangzíb's camp in the Deccan in 1695 throws light on an obscure portion of the reign. Catrou's *Histoire Générale de l'Empire du Mogol* (1715), founded on the Portuguese memoirs of 'M. Manouchi,' would be invaluable if there were any means of authenticating it by comparison with Manucci's MS.; as it is, the work is too full of errors, and savours too strongly of the *chronique scandaleuse* of some malicious and disappointed backstairs underling at the Mughal Court, to be esteemed as an authority. The contemporary Indian chroniclers, Kháfí Khán, Musta'idd Khán, 'Abd-al-Hamíd Láhorí, Ináyat Khán, Bakhtáwar Khán, and others, may be consulted in Elliot and Dowson's invaluable *History of India as told by its own Historians*, vol. vii. Elphinstone's *History of India* has been followed in its admirable account of the Deccan campaigns. All dates are given in New Style, and the varying spellings of Indian names have been reduced to uniformity. I have to express my gratitude to Sir William W. Hunter, who had originally undertaken this volume of the series, for making over to me in the most generous manner all the MS. materials which he had collected in India for this purpose.

S. L.-P.

CONTENTS

NOTE ON THE VOWEL SOUNDS

The orthography of proper names follows generally the system adopted by the Indian Government for the *Imperial Gazetteer of India*. That system, while adhering to the popular spelling of very well-known places, such as Punjab, Poona, Deccan, &c., employs in all other cases the vowels with the following uniform sounds :—

a, as in wom*a*n : *á*, as in f*a*ther : *i*, as in k*i*n : *í*, as in intr*i*gue : *o*, as in c*o*ld : *u*, as in b*u*ll : *ú*, as in r*u*le.

AURANGZÍB

INTRODUCTION

THE HERITAGE OF AKBAR

THE greatest of Indian rulers, the Emperor Akbar, died in 1605. Third in the succession of his dynasty, he was first in his genius for government the true founder of the Indian Empire of the Great Moguls. He left a magnificent heritage to his descendants. His realm embraced all the provinces of Hindústán, and included Kábul on the west, Bengal on the east, Kashmír beside the Himálayas, and Khándésh in the Deccan. He had not merely conquered this vast dominion in forty years of warfare, but he had gone far towards welding it into an organic whole. He united under one firm government Hindús and Muhammadans, Shí'a and Sunnís, Rájputs and Afgháns, and all the numerous races and tribes of Hindústán, in spite of the centrifugal tendencies of castes and creeds. In dealing with the formidable difficulties presented by the government of a peculiarly heterogeneous empire, he stands absolutely supreme among oriental sovereigns, and may even challenge comparison with the greatest of European kings. He was himself the spring and fount of the sagacious policy of his government, and the proof of the soundness of his system is the duration of his undiminished empire, in spite of the follies and vices of his successors, until it was undone by the puritan reaction of his great-grandson Aurangzíb.

Akbar's main difficulties lay in the diversity and jealousies of the races and religions with which he had to deal. It was his method of dealing with these difficulties which established the Mughal Empire in all the power and splendour that marked its sway for a hundred years to come. It was Aurangzíb's reversal of this method which undid his ancestor's work and prepared the way for the downfall of his dynasty.

Akbar had not studied the history of India in vain. He had realized from its lessons that, if his dynasty was to keep its hold on the country and withstand the onslaught of fresh hordes of invaders, it must rest on the loyalty of the native Hindús who formed the bulk of the population, supplied the quota of the army, and were necessarily entrusted with most of the civil employments. His aim was to found a national empire with the aid of a national religion. 'He accordingly constructed a State Religion, catholic enough, as he thought, to be acceptable to all his subjects. Such a scheme of a universal religion had, during two hundred years, been the dream of Hindú reformers, and the text of wandering preachers throughout India. On the death of the Bengal saint in the fifteenth century, the Muhammadans and Hindús contended for his body. The saint suddenly appeared in their midst, and, commanding them to look under the shroud, vanished. This they did: but under the winding-sheet they found only a heap of beautiful flowers, one half of which the Hindús burned with holy rites, while the other half was buried with pomp by the Musalmáns. In Akbar's time many sacred places had become common shrines for the two faiths: the Muhammadans venerating the same impression on the rocks as the footprint of their prophet, which the Hindús revered as the footprint of their god [1].'

The inscription written by the Emperor's friend and counsellor Abu-l-Fazl, for a temple in Kashmír, might serve as a motto for Akbar's creed:

> O God, in every temple I see people that see thee, and in every language I hear spoken, people praise thee.
> Polytheism and Islám feel after thee.
> Each religion says, 'Thou art one, without equal.'
> If it be a mosque, people murmur the holy prayer; and if it be a Christian Church, people ring the bell from love to thee.
> Sometimes I frequent the Christian cloister, and sometimes the mosque.
> But it is thou whom I seek from temple to temple.
> Thy elect have no dealings with heresy or with orthodoxy: for neither of them stands behind the screen of thy truth.
> Heresy to the heretic, and religion to the orthodox,
> But the dust of the rose-petal belongs to the heart of the perfume-seller.

He discarded the rigid tenets of Islám, and adopted

[1] Sir W. W. Hunter, *The Ruin of Aurangzeb*, 'Nineteenth Century,' May, 1887.

in their stead an eclectic pantheism, in which he incorporated whatever he found admirable in various creeds.

> 'I can but lift the torch
> Of Reason in the dusky cave of Life,
> And gaze on this great miracle, the World,
> Adoring That who made, and makes, and is,
> And is not, what I gaze on—all else, Form,
> Ritual, varying with the tribes of men[1].'

Akbar's State Religion was a failure. It never took hold of the people. No eclectic philosophy ever does. But his broad-minded sympathy drew the severed links of the empire together and for a while created a nation where there had been races. His watchword was Toleration. He was tolerant of all shades of religion and every tinge of nationality. He encouraged Portuguese Jesuits and admired their painted and graven images; he presided over philosophical discussions in which every received dogma was freely criticized; he sanctioned the worship of the sun, 'Symbol the Eternal,' as the most glorious manifestation of Deity, and would himself daily set the example to his people, and

> 'Kneel adoring Him the Timeless in the flame that measures Time.'

To carry out his public toleration in the privacy of home, he took his wives from different races and religions. All this was not done out of policy alone: he had a distinctly philosophical bent of thought. The practical side of this open-minded attitude was

[1] Tennyson, *Akbar's Dream* (1892), p. 33.

seen in the abolition of all taxes upon religious nonconformity. The detested *jizya* or Muhammadan poll-tax upon unbelievers, was done away. In the eyes of Akbar's tax-gatherer, as well as of his God, all men were equal, and nothing was 'common or unclean.' To conciliate the prejudices of race, he employed native Hindús, Persian heretics, and orthodox Afghán and Mughal Sunnís impartially in the offices of state and in the army, and conferred equal honours upon each denomination. To form the leading men of all races and creeds into one loyal corps, directly attached to the throne, he established a sort of feudal, but not hereditary, aristocracy, called *mansabdárs*, who were in receipt of salaries or held lands direct from the crown, during the pleasure of the sovereign, on condition of military service. The dangers of a possible territorial aristocracy, into which this body of life-peers might have developed, were minimized by a rigorous system of inspection and a careful supervision of the rent-collectors [1]. The system worked admirably so long as it was strictly carried out. For nearly a century Hindú and Persian nobles loyally served their common sovereign in war and in the civil government of the country. It broke down only when religious intolerance sapped its strength.

Akbar's son, Salím, who ascended the throne with the title of Jahángír, in October, 1605, at the age of

[1] See my *History of the Moghul Emperors illustrated by their Coins*, reprinted from the 'Catalogue of Indian Coins in the British Museum,' pp. xv ff., from which part of the present chapter is derived.

thirty-seven, offered a striking contrast to his incomparable father, against whom he had openly rebelled. His temper was violent and he was a notorious drunkard. In his astonishingly candid 'Memoirs,' he relates how (like his wretched brothers Murád and Dániyál) he had been addicted to intoxicating liquors from the age of eighteen, and used to drink as much as twenty cups a day, at first of wine, then of 'double-distilled liquor' of such potency that it made Sir Thomas Roe, the British ambassador, sneeze, to the delight of the whole Court. As he got older, he reduced his potations, but still was in the habit of becoming unconscionably muddled every night, insomuch that at supper he had to be fed by his servants, after which 'he turned to sleep, the candles were popped out,' says Sir Thomas, 'and I groped my way out in the dark.' But, sot as he was, Jahángír was no fool. He kept his orgies for the evening, and during the day he was sobriety personified. None of his nobles dared risk the faintest odour of wine at the daily levees; and an indiscreet reference to the 'obliterated' revels of the previous night was severely punished. The Emperor even went so far as to issue a virtuous edict against intemperance, and, like his contemporary James I, wrote a treatise against tobacco, though he said nothing about his favourite opium.

He must have inherited a splendid constitution from Akbar and his mother, a Rájput princess, for his debauchery does not seem to have materially injured his mind or body. Sir Thomas Roe formed a favourable opinion of his intelligence, and there can be no question that he displayed commendable energy in maintaining his authority throughout his wide dominions, in suppressing the rebellion of his eldest son, and in directing campaigns in the Deccan and against the Rájput chiefs. Jahángír cannot be credited, it is true, with the genius of initiative; but he was wise enough to continue the policy of his father, and this policy still retained the loyalty of the Hindús. His toleration arose more from indifference than from a liberal mind; but Muslim as he professed to be, he showed the same indulgence towards Hindús and Christians as Akbar had displayed. He too was a patron of Christian art: pictures and statues of the Madonna formed part of the decoration of his palaces. No doubt the success of his government was largely due to the abilities of his statesmen and generals; but the Emperor had wit and power enough to have taken his own line, if he had not preferred wisely to follow in the steps of his father. Towards the end of his reign, indeed, he fell completely under the influence of his imperious and gifted queen, the celebrated Núr-Jahán, who practically ruled the empire, with the aid of her brother, Ásaf Khán; and the effects of her sway were seen in the weakening of the old military spirit of the Mughals, the driving of the most capable of the Emperor's sons, Prince Khurram, into open rebellion, the increase of the pernicious practice of farming out the provincial governments, the spread of brigandage, and the monstrous cupidity of the Court in the matter of gifts. No one ever dreamt of coming to the Empress or her ministers empty-handed.

Jahángír died suddenly in November, 1627, at the age of fifty-eight, whilst on his way back from his usual summer visit to the refreshing valleys of Kashmír. After a brief delay, during which his grandson Búlákí was provisionally set on the throne with the title of Dáwar-Bakhsh, Prince Khurram assumed the sceptre at Agra in January, 1628, with the title of Sháh-Jahán, or 'King of the World.'

Like his father, Sháh-Jahán was the offspring of a union with a Rájput princess, a daughter of the proud Rája of Márwár, and had more Indian than Mughal blood in his veins. Yet he was a good Muhammadan of the orthodox Sunní profession, compared with his ancestors, and showed a tinge of intolerance which was wholly foreign to his easy-going father and broad-minded grandfather. His orthodoxy was fostered by the influence of his best-beloved wife, Mumtáz-Mahall, the mother of all his fourteen children, whose monument, erected by a devoted husband, is the famous Táj at Agra. But Sháh-Jahán was too prudent a king to let religion override statesmanship. He did not object to the presence of Jesuit missionaries, and, like Akbar, he employed Hindús to command his armies. The wars of his reign were unimportant: the Deccan was, as usual, a source of trouble, but the kingdoms of Bíjápúr and Golkonda were brought to temporary submission and compelled to pay tribute; and several campaigns were undertaken in the hope of recovering

Kandahár from the Persians. In these wars the Emperor's son Aurangzíb won his spurs.

The reign of Sháh-Jahán is notable chiefly for peaceful prosperity. His ministers were men of the highest ability. Sa'd-Alláh 'Allámí, a converted Hindú, was the most upright statesman of his age; and 'Alí Mardán and Âsaf Khán were men of approved integrity and energy. The French traveller Tavernier speaks of the gracious government of the Emperor as 'like that of a father over his family,' and bears witness to the security of the roads and the just administration of the law. A Hindú writer of the time vies with his Muhammadan and Christian contemporaries in extolling the equity of Sháh-Jahán's rule, his wise and liberal administration of the land, the probity of his courts of law, his personal auditing of the accounts, and the prosperity of the country resulting from all these causes.

The general tranquillity of the empire left Sháh-Jahán ample leisure to indulge in his favourite passion for display. To this day, his great works at Agra and his splendid palace at New Delhi testify to his grandiose conceptions of architecture. He christened his new city Sháhjahánábád, and for generations this was the only name given to Delhi on coins and in official documents. It was completed in 1648, after being ten years a-building, and, according to all accounts, it must have been the most magnificent palace on the face of the earth [1]. He is said to have

[1] See below, p. 93.

possessed a set of travelling tents, made in Kashmír, which took two months to pitch in succession. His coronation anniversaries were kept with the utmost splendour and extravagance. On these festivals he was weighed in the Mughal fashion against the precious metals, and bowls of costly jewels were poured over him, all of which, to the value of a million and a half, were ordered to be distributed to the people on the following day. Yet with all his magnificence, Sháh-Jahán was never arrogant. He discontinued the obnoxious ceremonial of prostration before the royal presence; and he was renowned for his kindness and benevolence, which endeared him to the people. No other Mughal Emperor was ever so beloved as Sháh-Jahán.

As he grew old, his benevolence and popularity did not decrease, but he abandoned himself more and more to pleasure, and allowed himself to be managed by his children. His favourite wife, the lady of the Táj, had died in 1631, in giving birth to their fourteenth child, and her husband had centred his affection upon his eldest daughter, Jahán-Ára, with so much fervour as to cause no little scandal, while he also denied himself none of the more transitory joys of the zenána. He had been a grave stern man in his prime, an energetic soldier, and a prudent counsellor: at the age of sixty-four he was a sensual pleasure-loving pageant of royalty, given over to ease and the delights of the eye:—

'Oh! had he still that Character maintain'd
Of Valour, which in blooming Youth he gain'd,
He promised in his East a glorious Race;
Now, sunk from his Meridian, sets apace.
But as the Sun, when he from Noon declines,
And with abated heat less fiercely shines,
Seems to grow milder as he goes away,
Pleasing himself with the remains of Day:
So he who, in his Youth, for Glory strove,
Would recompense his age with Ease and Love[1].'

The burden of state interfered with his enjoyment, and he sought to devolve his power upon his four sons, to each of whom he gave the viceroyalty of one of his distant provinces, in the hope of stilling their never-ending jealousies, and removing them from opportunities for unfilial ambition. The sceptre was falling from his hand, and he sought to secure peace for his old age by breaking it into pieces. The mistake soon became apparent. The fragments of the sceptre, like the rods of the Egyptian sorcerers, turned into so many serpents, which hissed about his throne, and strangled the remnant of his power, till the rod of Aurangzíb swallowed up the rest, and with them the Peacock Throne.

It was the tradition of Mughal monarchy that the dying eyes of the father should witness the rebellion of the son. Akbar had forgiven his undutiful heir Jahángír on his death-bed. Sháh-Jahán was himself in revolt when his parent died. It was now his turn to suffer the like fate. In 1657 he was afflicted with a malady which, in the words of Bernier, the ever

[1] Dryden, *Aureng-Zebe*, 'Constable's Oriental Miscellany,' vol. iii. (1892) p. 55.

polished French physician and traveller, 'it were unbecoming to describe.' The self-indulgence of the old sensualist had brought its retribution. It was generally feared that the disease would prove fatal: reports of his death were freely circulated, and each of the Princes at once prepared to fight for the crown:—

> 'As at a signal, streight the sons prepare
> For open force, and rush to sudden war:
> Meeting like winds broke loose upon the Main,
> To prove, by Arms, whose Fate it was to Reign.'

Whosesoever fate it should be, the new Emperor would have to confront different circumstances from his predecessors. Akbar's organization had welded an empire out of heterogeneous materials with marvellous success, but there were flaws in the work, which threatened to develop into serious cleavage. Toleration had bred indifference, and success had engendered luxury: the hardy troopers of Balkh had grown soft in the Capua of the Jamna, and their religious convictions had gone the way of the Deputy of Achaia. They had thrown away their old standard of manliness, and had become fops and epicures. Two of Akbar's sons died of drink, and the habit of intoxication had become so universal among the nobles and officials that even the chief Kází used to smuggle his daily dram into his house of a morning. In short, 'the heroic soldiers of the early empire, and their not less heroic wives, had given place to a vicious and delicate breed of grandees. The ancestors of

Aurangzíb, who swooped down on India from the north, were ruddy men in boots: the courtiers among whom Aurangzíb grew up were pale persons in petticoats. Bábar, the founder of the empire, had swum every river which he met with during thirty years' campaigning; the luxurious nobles around the youthful Aurangzíb wore skirts made of innumerable folds of the finest white muslin, and went to war in palankins.' The rough breath of their highland birth-place was changed to sickly essences; and the old battle-cry of Allah had become a hollow symbol of the religion they had studied to forget. Childish superstition or impotent indifference had taken the place of the old faith; and immorality and debauchery had followed close upon the loosening of the religious bond.

Against the Mughals—a term which by this time meant any Indian Muslim with a fair complexion, and implied very little Mughal blood—the new Emperor could set the Rájputs, the pick of the warriors of Hindústán, who had been loyal servants to three successive Mughal kings, but whose fidelity depended upon the respect paid to their prejudices and customs. They might either be the flower of the Imperial army, or its most formidable foe. The new Emperor had it in his power to decide which it should be.

To retrieve the growing effeminacy of the Mughals, to attach or curb the Rájputs, to check the tendency of provincial governors to transmit their prestige to their sons and found dynasties, to put a heart into a decaying system and a faith into a listless soul,—

such were the problems which confronted the son of Sháh-Jahán who should succeed to his father's splendid but cankering power. It was a task for a prophet like Muhammad, or such a king as Theodoric. The question was, should it be done by the zeal of the Lord, or by the compromise of the man of the world?

THE FAMILY OF AURANGZÍB.

TÍMÚR.
⋮
AKBAR,
b. 1542, *s.* 1556, *d.* 1605.
|
JAHÁNGÍR,
b. 1569, *s.* 1605, *d.* 1627.
|
SHÁH-JAHÁN.
b. 1592, *s.* 1627, *d.* 1666.

Jahán-Ará Begam Sáhib,	Dárá Shukóh,	Shujá',	*Raushan-Ará*,	AURANGZÍB Á'LAMGÍR	Murád-Bakhsh,	*Kudsiya*,
b. 1614, *d.* 1681.	*b.* 1615, *d.* 1659.	*b.* 1616, *d.* 1660.	*b.* 1617, *d.* 1671.	*b.* 4 Nov. 1618. *s.* July, 1658. *d.* 3 March 1707.	*b.* 1624, *d.* 1661.	*b.* 1630, *d.* 1706.

Children of Aurangzíb:

Zíb-an-Nisá.	Muhammad,	Mu'azzam SHÁH-'ÁLAM BAHÁDUR SHÁH	*Zínat-ar-Nisá*,	*Badr-an-Nisá*,	*Zubdat-an-Nisá*,	A'zam,	Akbar,	*Mihr-an-Nisá*,	Kám-Bakhsh
b. 1639, *d.* 1701.	*b.* 1639, *d.* 1676.	*b.* 1643, *s.* 1707, *d.* 1712.	*b.* 1643, *d.* 1708.	*b.* 1647, *d.* 1671.	*b.* 1651, *m.* Sipihr Shukóh, *d.* 1707.	*b.* 1653, *d.* 1708.	*b.* 1656 *d.* 1706.	*b.* 1661, *m.* son of Murád-Bakhsh, *d.* 1705.	*b.* 1667, *d.* 1709.

CHAPTER I

The Prince

The four sons of Sháh-Jahán who made ready in 1657 to fight for their apparently dying father's throne were Dárá the eldest, a man of forty-two, Shujá', a year younger, Aurangzíb, almost thirty-nine, and Murád-Bakhsh, the youngest, then in his thirty-fourth year[1]. Their characters have been drawn by Bernier, who knew Dárá and Aurangzíb personally, and acted as physician to each in succession. Dárá Shukóh, he tells us, was not wanting in good qualities, and could be both gracious and generous; but he was inordinately conceited and self-satisfied, very proud of his intellectual gifts, and extremely intolerant of advice and contradiction, which easily roused his imperious and violent Mughal temper. Though

[1] The translation of these names is Dárá, King; Shujá', Valiant; Aurangzíb, Throne-ornament; Murád-Bakhsh, Desire-attained. Sháh-Jahán had altogether fourteen children, all by his wife Mumtáz Mahall, whom he married in 1612, and who died in 1631. Six were girls and eight boys. Seven of them died in infancy; the names of those who grew up are given in the annexed pedigree, where the princesses are printed in italics. The Princess Kudsiya was apparently also known as Gohar-Ára.

nominally a Muhammadan in outward forms, he was really all things to all men, and prided himself on his breadth of view; accepting philosophical ideas from the Bráhmans who lived upon his bounty, and lending a sympathetic ear to the religious suggestions of the Reverend Father Buzée of the Company of Jesus. He wrote treatises on comparative theology, in which he maintained that 'infidelity' and Islám were almost twin sisters.

It has been suggested that Dárá's wide religious sympathies were assumed for political reasons, in order to win over the tributary Rájas, and the Christians who furnished all the best gunners for the artillery, with a view to the coming struggle for the throne: but it is more likely that he was honestly trying, according to his lights, to tread the path wherein Akbar had walked. As will be seen, Dárá's 'emancipated' ideas did him more harm than good, and formed a pretext for his destruction. But apart from his creed, or agnosticism, he was a nervous, sensitive, impulsive creature, full of fine feelings and vivid emotions, never master of himself or of others, and liable to lose his self-control just when cool judgement was most necessary. He might have been a poet or a transcendental philosopher; he could never have become a Ruler of India.

His next brother, Shujá', had more will and less elevation of character than Dárá. He was brave, discreet, subtle, and a dexterous diplomatist. He knew how to bribe the Hindú chiefs, and succeeded in interesting the great Mahárája of Márwár, Jaswant Singh, in his cause. He professed himself a Shí'í, or follower of 'Alí, in order to secure the adhesion of the powerful Persian lords. But he had a fatal weakness: 'he was too much a slave to his pleasures; and once surrounded by his women, who were exceedingly numerous, he would pass whole days and nights in dancing, singing, and drinking wine. He presented his favourites with rich robes, and increased or diminished their allowances as the passing fancy of the moment prompted. No courtier who consulted his own interest would attempt to detach him from this mode of life: the business of government [he was viceroy of Bengal] therefore often languished, and the affections of his subjects were in a great measure alienated[1].' It is recorded of the great Khalif Al-Mansúr, the true founder of the 'Abbásid empire, that when he was engaged in a war, he never looked upon the face of woman till he had triumphed. Shujá' might well have emulated his example. No Mughal sovereign who shut himself up in the seraglio, and neglected to show himself constantly to his subjects and listen to their complaints, had any chance of retaining his ascendancy over them. Shujá's zenána was the prison of his career.

Murád-Bakhsh, the youngest son of Sháh-Jahán, was a gallant swashbuckler, brave as a lion, frank

[1] Bernier, *Travels*, translated by Arch. Constable (1891), pp. 7, 8. To this edition, published as vol. i. of 'Constable's Oriental Miscellany,' all subsequent quotations from Bernier refer.

and open as the day; a fool in politics, a despiser of statecraft, and a firm believer in ruddy steel. He was the terror of the battle-field, and the best of good fellows over a bottle. No one could be better trusted in a melley; none was more fatuous in council or more reckless in a debauch. The hereditary passion for wine, which had descended from Bábar to his posterity, found a willing victim in this valiant boor. His name justified itself in accordance with his mental limitations: his 'desires' were indeed 'attained', but they were the sort of desires which lead to perdition.

Two princesses played an important part in the intrigues which circled round the sick-bed of their father. The elder, Jahán-Árá, or 'World-adorner,' known as Begam Sáhib, or Princess Royal, was her father's darling. Beautiful and 'of lively parts', she devoted herself to the solace of his old age, won his unbounded confidence, and, in the absence of any preëminent Queen, exerted unlimited influence in the Mughal Court. No intrigue or piece of jobbery could prosper without her aid, and the handsome presents she was always receiving from those who had anything to gain from the Emperor, added to her magnificent pin-money, made her extremely wealthy. She was condemned to the usual fate of Mughal princesses, the state of single blessedness, because no alliance in India was considered worthy of the Princess Royal, or because no great Lord cared to burden himself with the oppressive glory of becoming the husband of an imperious wife. Princesses did not conduce to domestic peace in a polygamous household. The Princess Royal is said, however, like some other *grandes et honnêtes dames de par le monde*, to have consoled herself. In politics, she was a warm ally of Dárá, and exerted all her influence with the King on his behalf. Her younger sister, Raushan-Árá, or 'Brilliant Ornament,' on the other hand, was a staunch supporter of Aurangzíb, and cordially hated the Princess Royal and her eldest brother. So long as Dárá lived, she had little power, but she watched zealously over Aurangzíb's interests, and kept him constantly informed of all that went on at Court. She was not so handsome as her sister; but this did not prevent her having her little affairs, without which a spinster's life in the zenána had few distractions.

Aurangzíb, the third son of Sháh-Jahán, was born on the night of the 4th of November, 1618, at Dhúd, on the borders of Málwa, nearly half-way between Baroda and Ujjain. His father was at that time Viceroy of the Deccan province, but the future emperor was only two years old when Sháh-Jahán fell into disgrace with the Court, and was forced to fly, fighting the while, through Telingána and Bengal, and three or four years passed before he could again resume his place in the Deccan. At last he offered his submission and apologies to Jahángír, and was allowed to remain undisturbed, on condition that he sent two of his sons, Dárá and Aurangzíb, as hostages to the Court at Agra (1625). Nothing is known of the life of the child during the years of civil war, or of his captivity under the jealous eyes of Queen Núr-Jahán. Nor is anything recorded of his boyhood, from the day when, at the age of nine, he saw his father ascend the throne, to the year 1636, when the youth of seventeen was appointed to the important office of Governor of the Deccan. The childhood of an eastern prince is usually uneventful. Aurangzíb doubtless received the ordinary education of a Muslim, was taught his Korán, and well grounded in the mysteries of Arabic grammar and the various scholastic accomplishments which still make up the orthodox body of learning in the East. He certainly acquired a facility in verse, and the prose style of his Persian letters is much admired in India. In later years he complained of the narrow course of study set before him by his ignorant—or at least conventional—tutor [1], and drew a sketch of what the education of a Prince ought to be. To his early religious training, however, he probably owed his decided bent towards Muslim puritanism, which was at once his distinction and his ruin.

Aurangzíb's early government of the Deccan was a nominal rule. The young prince seems to have been more occupied with thoughts of the world to come than with measures for the subjugation of the earth beneath his eyes. Possibly the pomp and empty pageantry of his father's sumptuous Court set the earnest young mind thinking of the 'vanity of human wishes'; or some judicious friend may have instilled

[1] See below, p. 76.

into the receptive soul the painful lessons to be drawn from the careless self-indulgence of too many of his royal relatives. Whatever the influence, it is clear that he had early learnt to look upon life as a serious business. In 1643, when only twenty-four, he announced his intention of retiring from the world, and actually took up his abode in the wild regions of the Western Ghâts (where Dr. Fryer was shown his retreat) and adopted the rigorous system of self-mortification which distinguished the fakír or mendicant friar of Islám.

This extraordinary proceeding, far more bizarre in a youthful Mughal prince than in the elderly, gouty, and disappointed Emperor Charles V, has been set down by some of his critics to Aurangzíb's subtle calculation and hypocrisy. It is insinuated that the pretence of indifference to the seductions of power was designedly adopted with a view to hoodwink his contemporaries as to his real ambition. There is, however, no reasonable ground for the insinuation, which is but one of many instances of the way in which Aurangzíb's biographers have ridden to death their theory of his duplicity. So far from proving of service to him, his choice of a life of devotion only drew down his father's severe wrath. The Prince was punished by the stopping of his pay, the loss of his rank and estates, and his deposition from the governorship of the Deccan. His own family were undoubtedly impressed with his religious character, and his eldest brother Dárá, with the superior air of an 'emancipated' agnostic, called him 'that saint'; but it remains to be proved that they were deceived in their estimate of their brother,—a rare experience among close relations,—or that his accepted *rôle* as a devotee raised his character in the estimation of either the nobles or the people. Moreover, had he been so deeply designing an impostor, he would have played his part so long as was necessary to develop his plans; he would have waited till the opportunity came to strike, for which he was watching in his lonely cell. Instead of this, in a year's time Aurangzíb was out of his seclusion, exercising all the powers of a Viceroy in the important province of Gújarát. Henceforward we shall see him always to the fore when war was going on, keeping himself steadily before the eyes of the people. The truth seems to be that his temporary retirement from the world was the youthful impulse of a morbid nature excited by religious enthusiasm. The novelty of the experiment soon faded away; the fakír grew heartily tired of his retreat; and the young Prince returned to carry out his notions of asceticism in a sphere where they were more creditable to his self-denial, and more operative upon the great world in which he was born to work. He was not destined to be a

> 'Deedless dreamer, lazying out a life
> Of self-suppression:'

his ascetic mind was fated to influence the course of an empire.

The youthful dream was soon dispelled, and the

erewhile fakír became a statesman and a leader of armies. In February, 1647, Sháh-Jahán raised him to the rank of a *mansabdár* of 15,000 personal and 10,000 horse, and ordered him to take command of the provinces of Balkh and Badakhshán, on the north-west side of the Hindú Kúsh, which had lately been added to the Mughal Empire. They had once been the dominion of Bábar, the grandfather of Akbar, and it had long been the ambition of Sháh-Jahán to assert his dormant claim and recover the territory of his renowned ancestor. He even aspired to use these provinces as stepping-stones to the recovery of the ancient kingdom of Samarkand, once the capital of a still earlier and more famous ancestor, Tímúr, the 'Scourge of God.' This kingdom, with the dependent provinces of Balkh and Badakhshán, now belonged to the Uzbegs, who were governed by a member of the Astrakhán dynasty, ultimately descended, like their Indian antagonists, from Jinghiz Kaán. Their sway, however, was but a shadow of the power which Tamerlane had bequeathed to his successors; and the Persian general 'Alí Mardán, accompanied by the youngest Imperial Prince, Murád-Bakhsh, at the head of 50,000 horse and 10,000 foot and artillery, had accomplished, though not without severe fighting, the conquest of Balkh and the neighbouring cities in 1645.

The difficulty, however, was not so much how to take, but how to keep, this distant region, separated by the snowy ranges of the Hindú Kúsh from the rest of the Empire, inaccessible in winter, and exposed at all times to the attack of the indomitable hill tribes, who have always made the government of the mountain region a thankless task to every ruler who has attempted to subdue them. When Aurangzíb reached the scene of his government, he soon perceived the character of the country and its defenders, and like a wise general counselled a retreat from an untenable position. He made terms with the King of the Uzbegs, restored the useless provinces, and began his march home. It was now October, and no time was to be lost in re-crossing the mountains. A long scene of disaster ensued, though Aurangzíb, in concert with his Persian and Indian advisers, took every precaution, and personally superintended the movement. The hill men hovered about the flanks of the retreating Rájputs, cut off detached parties, and harassed every step. The baggage fell over precipices; the Hazaras bristled above the narrow defiles; the Hindú Kúsh was under snow, which fell for five days; and 5000 men, to say nothing of horses, elephants, camels, and other beasts of burden, died from cold and exposure. It was but a dejected frostbitten remnant of the army that reached Kábul; and Sháh-Jahán's precious scheme of aggrandizement had cost the exchequer more than two million pounds.

Aurangzíb's next employment was equally unsuccessful. Kandahár, which had belonged to the Sháh of Persia, had been surrendered to the Mughals ten years before (1637) by its able and ambitious governor, 'Alí Mardán, who speedily wiped out his treachery to the old master by distinguished services to the new, not only in war, but in such works of peace as the well-known canal at Delhi, which still bears his name. Towards the close of 1648 the Persians besieged the city, and Aurangzíb and the great minister, Sa'd-Allah 'Allámí, accompanied by Rája Jai Singh and his Rájputs, were sent to relieve it. The Mughal army numbered 60,000 horse and 10,000 infantry and artillery. Before they reached Kábul, however, Kandahár had fallen; and measures were accordingly taken for a siege. In May, 1649, the Mughals opened their batteries, and mines and countermines, sallies and assaults, went on with great vigour for four months. The army, however, had come for a pitched battle, not for a siege, and there were no heavy guns. By September little progress had been made, and the winter was coming on. Aurangzíb had experienced one winter retreat in the mountains, and he would not risk a second. The army retired to Kábul.

In the spring of 1652, another attempt was made to recover Kandahár, and Aurangzíb was again sent with Sa'd-Allah, at the head of an army 'like the waves of the sea,' with a siege-train, including eight heavy and twenty light guns, and 3000 camels carrying ammunition. But the frontiers were strong and vigorously defended; the besiegers' guns were badly served, and two of them burst; the enemy's sallies and steady fire drove back the engineers; and after two months and eight days the siege was again abandoned.

Nor was an even more determined leaguer by Prince Dárá early in the following year any more successful, though some of his ordnance projected shot of nearly a hundredweight.

These campaigns in Afghánistán and beyond the Hindú Kúsh are of no importance in the history of India, except as illustrating the extreme difficulty of holding the mountain provinces from a distant centre, whether it be Delhi or Calcutta; but they were of the greatest service to Aurangzíb. They put him in touch with the imperial army, and enabled him to prove his courage and generalship in the eyes of the best soldiers in the land. It is not to be supposed that, with tried commanders like 'Alí Mardán, Jai Singh, and Sa'd-Allah, at his side, Aurangzíb enjoyed the real command. He was doubtless at first more a nominal than an acting general,—a princely figure-head to decorate the war-ship of proved officers. But as time went on, opportunities occurred for the exercise of his personal courage and tactical skill. The generals learnt to appreciate him at his true value, and the men discovered that their Prince was as cool and steady a leader as the best officer in India. When they saw him, in the midst of a battle with the Uzbegs, at the hour of evening prayer, calmly dismounting and performing his religious rites under fire, they recognised the mettle of the man. Henceforth every soldier and statesman in Hindústán knew that, whatever time should bring forth in the future of the empire, Aurangzíb was a factor to be reckoned with.

He had gone over the mountains an unknown quantity, a reputed devotee, with no military record to give him prestige. He came back an approved general, a man of tried courage and powers of endurance, a prince whose wisdom, coolness and resolution had been tested and acclaimed in three arduous campaigns. The wars over the north-west frontier had ended as such wars have often ended since, but they had done for Aurangzíb what they did for Stewart and Roberts; they placed their leader in the front rank of Indian generals. After Balkh and Kandahár, the Prince was recognized as the coming man.

CHAPTER II

THE FIGHT FOR THE THRONE

THE inevitable destiny of a prince who had displayed such ability and energy in the campaigns in Afghánistán was to govern the ever-disturbed province of the Deccan. The record of what Aurangzíb did there in 1655–7 will find its place in a later chapter[1]; here it suffices to say that his dealings with the Muhammadan kingdoms of Golkonda and Bíjápúr added greatly to his renown both as a general and as a diplomatist. In the midst of his successes, he was called away to face the crisis of his life. In the autumn of 1657, as has already been related, his father, Sháh-Jahán, was reported to be sick unto death. A fratricidal struggle for the crown at once began, in which Aurangzíb took the principal part. It was no child's play, for all the four brothers were mature men of fixed characters and definite aims, and each had had experience in the art of war and in the government of provinces. Their father, remembering his own contumacy towards Jahángír, and ever

[1] See below, pp. 147–151.

fearful of civil war and unfilial ambition, had endeavoured to minimize their jealousy and power for mischief by appointing them Viceroys of provinces as distant as possible from the capital and from each other. Shujá' was away to the east, Governor of Bengal; Aurangzíb was down south in the Deccan; Murád-Bakhsh was in the west, making merry in the capacity of Viceroy of Gújarát. Dárá, the eldest, was assigned the government of Multán and of distant Kábul, but had become so necessary to his father that he deputed his functions to others, and himself remained at Delhi attached to the King's person. Each of the princes behaved more like an independent sovereign than a lieutenant of the Emperor. They had the command of large revenues, which they devoted to the formation of large armies in preparation for the struggle which they knew to be inevitable.

Dárá was apparently the favourite, and as the Emperor grew older his eldest son's influence increased. After the last desperate assault upon Kandahár, the prince had received many marks of his father's regard. He was given the title of Sháh Baland Ikbál, 'Lord of Exalted Fortune,' and invested with a robe of honour studded with diamonds and pearls, said to be worth 50,000 rupees (£5600), and a splendid ruby for his turban, besides other jewels and money to the value of a third of a million. Most significant of all, a golden couch had been placed for him below the imperial throne, and Dárá, alone of all the royal family, was allowed to be seated in the presence of the King. No clearer sign was needed to show the Court that Sháh-Jahán intended his eldest son to succeed him. When the King's dangerous illness withdrew him from the management of affairs, it was naturally Dárá who took his place. In so doing he was within his rights as eldest son and presumptive heir to the crown of Delhi. But he knew he had to reckon with three brothers, each at the head of an army and in command of a province, and the measures he took to prevent the news of his father's illness reaching them show that he dreaded the consequences of his assumption of royal functions. A singular light is cast upon the instability of the imperial organization when it is remembered that no Mughal king dared to absent himself from the public levees for more than a day or two, for fear of a general rebellion. The people were satisfied only if they could see their king: if he were not seen he must be dead. Even Jahángír, after his nightly debauch, had to 'pull himself together,' *coûte que coûte*, and make his punctual appearance at the levee window. Sháh-Jahán's absence from his accustomed seat overlooking the great Hall of Audience could not fail to arouse suspicion, and the rumour that he was dead, in spite of Dárá's assurances, spread rapidly throughout the provinces, and every man looked to his weapons and made ready for the fray. Bernier describes the tumult of this anxious time:—

'The Mughal's illness filled the whole extent of his dominions with agitation and alarm. Dárá collected powerful armies in Delhi and Agra, the principal cities of the kingdom. In Bengal, Sultán Shujá' made the same vigorous preparations for war. Aurangzíb in the Deccan and Murád-Bakhsh in Gújarát also levied such forces as evinced a determination to contend for empire. The four brothers gathered round them their friends and allies; all wrote letters, made large promises, and entered into a variety of intrigues . . . Meanwhile the King's distemper increased, and it was reported that he was dead. The whole Court was in confusion; the population of Agra was panic-stricken; the shops were closed for many days; and the four Princes openly declared their settled purpose of making the sword the sole arbiter of their lofty pretensions. It was, in fact, too late to recede: not only was the crown to be gained by victory alone, but in case of defeat life was certain to be forfeited. There was now no choice but between a kingdom and death.'

Sháh Shujá', the second son, was the first in the field. He at once announced that his father had been poisoned by Dárá; proclaimed himself Emperor; engraved his name on the coinage of Bengal, and set out to march upon Agra. Sháh-Jahán hastened to reassure him on the score of his health: but Shujá' declined to believe the good news. Almost at the same moment Murád-Bakhsh caused his coins to be struck at Ahmadábád and the Prayer for the King to be recited in his own name, and displayed his lordly instinct by immediately assaulting the city of Súrat and extorting six lacs of rupees from its luckless merchants. Aurangzíb, alone of the four brothers, assumed no royal function. Whatever his designs may have been, he kept them to himself. It is possible that as yet he did not know them, but was led on by the hazard of events. At any rate he played a waiting game. He knew the impetuosity of Dárá, the sluggish inertness of Shujá', and the careless, happy-go-lucky disposition of his truculent youngest brother. He let them push themselves forward, and waited for the upshot. He did not declare himself even when he heard that Dárá had seized his house and imprisoned his agent at Delhi. But he must have known that the accession of any of his brothers meant death or captivity for himself, and his mind must soon have been made up. In self-defence he was bound to make his bid for power, and once this was determined, it only remained to choose the line of action. Others, like Murád-Bakhsh and Shujá', might strike boldly at their quarry: Aurangzíb ever loved to stalk it by circuitous paths. His genius lay in diplomatic craft, and his approach to the throne was made by roundabout curves and zigzags.

Dárá was prompt in asserting his authority. He lost no time in sending out the imperial armies to chastise Shujá' and Murád-Bakhsh. In December, 1657, he despatched his own son, Sulaimán Shukóh, under the tutorship of Rája Jai Singh, to suppress Shujá'; whilst the Mahárája Jaswant Singh of Márwár, assisted by Kásim Khán, marched to meet the advance of Murád-Bakhsh, with instructions to cut the line of communication between the rebel viceroy of Gújarát and his wary brother of the Deccan. Dárá was more anxious about Aurangzíb's movements than the others, but he feared to let Shujá' approach the capital and possibly seize the person of Sháh-Jahán, who was the key of the situation. His forces were so large that he thought he might safely divide them. The result proved that he had committed a false move. He had better have left Shujá' alone for a while, and concentrated all his resources upon the task of crushing Aurangzíb. Shujá', it is true, was easily repulsed. Jai Singh surprised him at his camp near Benáres, and attacked before sun-rise, while the careless *bon vivant* was yet heavy with wine. After a brief contest the rebels gave way, and the dazed Prince, hardly awake, hastily took to flight, leaving his camp and treasure, artillery and ammunition, in the hands of Dárá's officers. The pursuit was merely perfunctory, for Sháh-Jahán had strictly enjoined leniency towards his rebellious son.

Meanwhile Aurangzíb pursued his policy of playing a strictly subordinate part. He wrote to congratulate Murád-Bakhsh on his successful capture of Súrat, and added, 'Whatever course you have resolved upon in opposition to the shameless and unrighteous conduct of our abandoned brother, you may count on me as a staunch ally. Our father is still alive, and we two are bound to come to his aid, and punish the presumption and pride of the apostate.' He threw out hints, quite after his puritan ideas, that after restoring order, they should try to reclaim the malignant and send him on a pilgrimage to Mecca. He urged an immediate advance against 'that presumptuous infidel Jaswant Singh,' promised to join the army of Gújarát on the north of the Narbadá, and ended by invoking 'the Word of God as his bail for this compact.' Still more to the purpose, he sent a lac of rupees[1] as earnest of his sincerity. Aurangzíb's policy was actuated as much perhaps by hatred of Dárá and the dread of his tyranny, as by personal ambition. The eldest Prince had used his influence with Sháh-Jahán to thwart his brother's plans in the Deccan, had restricted his powers, countermanded his campaigns, and placed the Persian Jumla, formerly a distinguished officer of the King of Golkonda, in supreme command of the army of the south. Fortunately for Aurangzíb, the Amír showed himself devoted to his cause, and allowed the Prince to lead the whole Deccan army to meet the imperial host.

At the end of March, 1658, Aurangzíb left Burhánpúr on his progress to the capital. His younger brother joined him near the Narbadá, and towards the close of April the combined forces came upon the enemy near Dharmátpúr in the territory of Ujjain. The invalid Emperor at Agra had sent repeated messages to Aurangzíb, assuring him of his convalescence, and commanding him to retire to his government in the south. But the brothers knew it was too late to go back; they pretended, or perhaps really

[1] The rupee at that time was worth 2s. 3*d*. The lac (*lakh*) is 100,000 rupees (£11,250), and the crore (*karór*) 100 lacs, or 10,000,000 rupees (£1,125,000).

believed, that the Emperor's letters were forged by Dárá; they declared that their father was either dead or dying, and they announced their determination, if he were still living, to throw themselves at his feet and deliver him from the tyranny of 'the apostate.' In accordance with this resolve, which may have been genuine, Aurangzíb sent a Bráhman orator to the Mahárája Jaswant Singh with a message to this effect: 'I desire to visit my father. I do not wish for war. Either come with me, or keep out of my way, that no blood be shed.' The Rájput returned an insulting reply, and both sides made ready for battle.

The accounts of the engagement of the 25th of April are in many respects conflicting. It is evident that Sháh-Jahán's temporizing policy, and possibly Aurangzíb's promises and bribes, had divided the counsels of the generals. Some were for carrying out Dárá's furious orders and exterminating the rebels; others paid heed to his father's command to deal gently with the misguided princes. Had Jaswant Singh attacked as soon as Aurangzíb appeared on the opposite bank of the Narbadá, the history of the Mughal empire might have been turned into a different channel. Dárá as Emperor might have played the part of a lesser Akbar; the Hindú element might have become supreme in India; and a united kingdom, dominated by Rájput chiefs, might have offered a stubborn resistance to the encroachments of the English traders. But Sháh-Jahán, in his weak desire to play off the ability of Aurangzíb against the overbearing pretentions of Dárá, had ordered his troops merely to dispute the passage of the river, not to cross to the attack. The enemy was thus allowed two precious days in which to bring up his entire forces, and when Murád-Bakhsh at length rode over the ford, under a withering storm of arrows and javelins, the whole strength of the Deccan followed, and crashed into the royal army with an overwhelming shock. Kásim Khán and his Muhammadans fled from the field like traitors or politicians. The Rájputs fought desperately, till only 600 remained out of their 8000 men. The wounded remnant sadly followed their Rája back to his desert fastness in Márwár. There he was received with bitter scorn. His high-mettled wife shut the castle gates in his face, saying that a man so dishonoured should not enter her walls. 'I disown him as my husband: these eyes can never again behold him. If he could not vanquish, he should die.' This was the true Rájput spirit, and the fact that the princess eventually became reconciled to her husband only proves that, though a daughter of the proud house of Chitór, she was, after all, a woman.

The Mughal capital was in an uproar. All sorts of plans were devised and rejected. Sháh-Jahán wished to go himself at the head of his army to confront the insurgents, and had he done so the issue might have been different; for his sons would hardly have ventured to attack him, lest their own troops should desert them for the standard of their revered Emperor. But Dárá was full of rage at the defeat of Jaswant

Singh, and resolved to wipe out the disgrace by a victory which should glorify his own name. He wanted no one to share his coming triumph. He would not even wait for his son Sulaimán Shukóh and the victorious army of Bengal, lest he should find an ambitious partner in his exploit. He longed for a personal glory such as the mighty Rameses recorded in the proud inscription which we read on the pylons of Karnak: 'The princes and captains joined not hands with me in fight. By Myself have I done battle. I have put to flight thousands of the nations: *and I was alone!*' But there were other and better reasons for Dárá's precipitate attack. The enemy were exhausted by long marches; they had not then crossed the Chambal; and the imperial army was more than strong enough to crush the jaded invaders as they struggled across a rapid ford. Moreover, every day's delay was an encouragement to the enemy, and an opportunity for Sháh-Jahán to exercise his fatal bent for diplomacy. If the blow were not struck now, it might never be struck at all.

The Emperor was too weak to resist his son's eager importunity. He let him go, with tears. Had he forbidden, it would have been useless, for the troops were under Dárá's orders, and knew his violent temper too well to disobey him. The lowest calculation places his army at 100,000 horse, 20,000 foot, and 80 guns; but the unpopularity of their headstrong commander, and the growing belief in the Puritan's fortune, bred traitors in the camp. Aurangzíb openly boasted that he had 30,000 adherents among the enemy, and the result showed at least that there were many half-hearted fighters in their ranks. The prophets were gloomy; no one presaged success for the Crown Prince; the temper of his troops was not that of men going to victory.

Heedless of these ominous forecasts, and full of the lust of personal *éclat*, such as he had sought and missed at Kandahár, Dárá led a splendid array to the encounter. On arriving at the Chambal, he found that Aurangzíb had given him the slip, and making a circuit had crossed the river on the 2nd of June, in spite of the imperial outposts. The two armies came in sight of each other on the 7th, at Samúgarh, afterwards known as Fathábád, 'The place of victory.' For a day or more they remained observing one another. The heat was such as is only known on the plains of India. It was a true Agra summer, and the men were fainting and dying in their heavy armour. During the pause, letters came from the Emperor, announcing the near approach of the Bengal army, and urging Dárá to wait for this reinforcement. His answer was characteristic: Before three days he would bring his brothers, bound hand and foot, to receive their father's judgment.

Early in the morning, or in Persian metaphor 'when the sun, the mighty monarch of the golden crown, with his world-conquering sword, rose brightly refulgent from his eastern bed, and the king of the starry host put his head out of the window of the horizon,' Aurangzíb marshalled his men. Keeping the command of the centre for himself, he placed Murád-Bakhsh in the left wing, appointed Bahádur Khán to lead the right, and sent forward his own son Muhammad with the advance guard to act with the artillery, which were, as usual, in the van. Dárá meanwhile disposed his forces in a similar order. He placed his cannon in front, linked together by iron chains, so that the enemy's cavalry might not break through. Immediately behind the cannon, he ranged a line of light artillery-camels, mounting brass pieces worked on swivels, and fired by the rider. Then came infantry armed with muskets. The mass of the army was composed, as usual, of cavalry, armed with sabres, pikes, and arrows. The last was the favourite weapon of the Mughals and Persians; the hand-pike being the special arm of the Rájputs. Khalíl-Allah Khán commanded the right, Rustam Khán the left, and Dárá himself was with the centre.

The battle began, as Mughal battles always did, by an artillery engagement; cannon were fired; rockets or hand-grenades were thrown to create a stampede among the enemy's horses and elephants; and then the infantry came into action with their clumsy matchlocks, whilst flights of arrows flew over their heads from the archers behind. Dárá's advance guard, under his son Sipihr Shukóh, then came out and drove in Prince Muhammad's squadrons, and this advantage was immediately followed up by bringing the left wing to bear upon Aurangzíb's right, which wavered, and seemed on the point of breaking, when reinforcements opportunely came up from the centre. After this the engagement became general. Dárá, towering high above his horsemen on a beautiful Ceylon elephant, led his centre against Aurangzíb, carried the enemy's guns, after severe loss, and routed the camel corps and infantry. With the shock of horsemen against horsemen the real struggle began. No Mughal Prince, as yet, knew the colour of the 'white feather,' and Dárá displayed all the splendid valour of his famous blood. Emptying their quivers upon the Deccan horse, he and his men came to the sword, and fought hand to hand till the enemy began to break and fly.

It was the critical moment of the fight. The day was going against Aurangzíb. The flower of his cavalry was driven back, and he was now standing with scarcely a thousand men about him, awaiting Dárá's onslaught. Never was cool courage put to a severer test: but Aurangzíb's nerve was steel. '*Dilí*, *Yárána*, Take heart, my friends,' he cried. '*Khuda-hé*! There is a God! what hope have we in flight? Know ye not where is our Deccan? *Khuda-hé*! *Khuda-he*!' Thereupon he ordered the legs of his elephant to be chained together, to make retreat impossible. The mere order was enough to restore the ebbing courage of the few squadrons that still stood beside him.

A fortunate distraction at this instant diverted

Dárá's attack. Instead of annihilating Aurangzíb, he went to support his own left wing which had at length been repulsed by the enemy's right, and thus he lost the best chance that fate ever threw in his way.

Meanwhile Murád-Bakhsh was hotly engaged with Dárá's right, and was fighting like a lion and reeking with slaughter. Three thousand Uzbegs charged up to his ensanguined elephant, and arrows, spears, and battle-axes rained so thickly that the frightened animal turned to fly. The Mughal courage was again put to the test. The elephant's legs were quickly chained. Then Rája Rám Singh, of the valiant Rantela stock, came riding up with his Rájputs, insolently shouting, 'Dost *thou* dispute the throne with Dárá Shukóh?' and hurling his spear at the Prince, tried to cut his elephant's girths. The Mughal, wounded as he was, and sore beset on all hands, cast his shield over his little son, who sat beside him in the howdah, and shot the Rája dead. The fallen Rájputs, in yellow garb, and stained with their warpaint of turmeric, were heaped about the elephant's feet, and 'made the ground yellow as a field of saffron.' In another part of the field, the Ráhtor Rája Rúp Singh sprang from his horse, and having 'washed his hands of life,' cut his way through the Mughals, and throwing himself beneath the elephant strove to cut the girths of Aurangzíb's howdah. The Prince had enough to do to hold his own without this desperate assault; but he found time to admire the gallant attempt with disinterested coolness, and bade his followers take the daring Ráhtor alive—too late.

The cool courage of the one Prince and the fiery valour of the other daunted Dárá's division. The Rájputs had been slain in heaps, many of their chiefs were dead, and now Rustam, the commander of the imperial left wing, had fallen in rallying his men to one more spirited charge. The advantage was still on the side of the Agra army, and Aurangzíb and Murád-Bakhsh were perilously hemmed in by raving Rájputs, maddened with *bang*, and furious at the death of their chiefs: but it needed little to turn the balance of fortune either way. It was Dárá's unlucky destiny always to turn it against himself. At this crisis he committed the most fatal error that an Indian commander could perpetrate. All the army looked to his tall elephant as to a standard of victory. Yet now, when the day seemed almost his own, he must need dismount. He may have been alarmed at the rocket which just then struck his howdah, or listened to the treacherous counsel of Khalíl-Alláh, the commander of the right wing, who had chosen to consider himself held in reserve, and had looked on with his 30,000 Mughal troops without stirring a finger in the fight. Whatever impelled him, Dárá descended. Murád-Bakhsh was still there on his gory elephant, with his howdah stuck as full of arrows as a porcupine with quills, grimly dealing blow for blow and shaft for shaft.

Aurangzíb towered high above a seething scrimmage of Rájputs. But where was Dárá?

It was as though the sun had vanished in mid heaven. Dárá is dead, cried one; we are betrayed, said another: Aurangzíb will have vengeance, thought all. A blind panic seized upon the all but victorious army, and every man fled for dear life. Once a panic has got hold of an Indian army, no power can save or check it. Like a river which has burst its banks, it pours over the land, and none may dam or guide its widening waves. In a brief moment the tide had turned, and the all but vanquished became the victors. For a terrible quarter of an hour Aurangzíb had steadily maintained his seat on his besieged elephant, and his reward was the Peacock-Throne. A little too soon Dárá had dismounted, to be 'numbered among the most miserable of Princes,' a fugitive and a vagabond in the earth. The unlucky Prince, 'prizing life more than the hope of a crown,' turned and fled. A few of his once superb host followed him to Agra. Then, and not till then, did Aurangzíb descend from his elephant, and prostrating himself on the bloody field offered thanks to God for this great and glorious victory.

'Nothing succeeds like success.' The battle of Samúgarh was the signal for all the world to come and tender their homage to Aurangzíb, who remained for some days on the field of his triumph, busily engaged night and day in negotiating with his father's Amírs. They required little inducement to come over to the side of the rising man. It was an instructive and lamentable sight to behold them trooping to the new colours, totally unmindful of the old Emperor, who with all his senile faults had been a kind and generous master. Among those who offered Aurangzíb their services was his uncle, the Khán-Jahán Sháyista Khán, son of the late minister Ásaf Khán, and brother of the Queen Mumtáz-Mahall. He had already used his great influence with the Emperor on behalf of his successful nephew, and Sháh-Jahán was persuaded to mingle paternal reproof with conciliatory overtures. He sent his triumphant son a sword engraved with the auspicious name *'Álamgír*, 'world-compeller.' The Rája Jai Singh, who commanded the army which had successfully repulsed Shujá' in Bengal, was quickly advised of Dárá's fall, and gave in his adhesion to the coming man. The Mahárája Jaswant Singh, burying the hatchet, presently followed his example, and tendered his fealty to the new power.

Fortified by these signs of support, Aurangzíb turned his attention to his most dangerous rival, the still popular Sháh-Jahán. Dárá had already fled with a few hundred followers, and his father had sent money and 5000 horsemen to assist him. It was evident that the Emperor's sympathies were with his vanquished son, whatever he may have written in the futile hope of throwing dust in the eyes of the very clear-sighted victor. Aurangzíb was not deceived; he had taken his father's measure with great accuracy, and never intended to give him another chance. Sháh-Jahán had missed his opportunity when he was dissuaded from putting himself at the head of Dárá's army and compelling the submission of the opposing forces, who were still loyal to their Emperor. He missed it again when he neglected to come out in state, surrounded by his nobles and retinue, and compel the filial homage of his sons on the field of their victory. The luxurious old epicure had lost his chances, and exposed his weakness of purpose. To restore such a man to power meant the recall of Dárá and the revival of the horrors of civil war. Even to be friendly with him, and visit him in his palace, was to court assassination at the hands of the imperial guards, or the 'large and robust' Tatar amazons of the seraglio—so Aurangzíb was warned by his faithful sister Raushan-Árá. There was but one possible course: the weak-kneed Emperor must be made a prisoner. The trap which Sháh-Jahán laid, to ensnare his son to his ruin, caught the old king himself. Instead of Aurangzíb coming to be murdered, his son Muhammad entered the fortress on the 18th June, 1658, overcame the guard, and turned the palace into a prison. Aurangzíb pretended, in his excess of political prudence, that the detention was only temporary, and that he hoped to see his father again restored to power as soon as the evil machinations of Dárá should be finally suppressed. But this was mere talk, intended to reconcile the people to the deposition of a popular sovereign: and it must be allowed that they were very speedily consoled. Sháh-

Jahán never left the fortress of Agra during the seven years of life that remained to him. At first a bitter correspondence widened the breach between the captive and his jailor, and Sháh-Jahán had the baseness to try to corrupt Prince Muhammad and induce him to raise his standard against his father. But the Prince knew Aurangzíb, and did not feel sure of his grandfather, so the experiment failed. After this Sháh-Jahán became gradually more reconciled to his captivity, and Aurangzíb did all that was possible to mitigate his distress. He was allowed every enjoyment that his sensuous nature demanded, loaded with presents, and supplied with such amusements as most entertained him. His daughter, the Begam Sáhib, and all his numerous women, kept him company. Cooks skilfully ministered to his appetite, and dancers and singing girls enlivened his senile revels. Like many another aged voluptuary, he became wondrously devout at times, and holy Mullas came and read the blessed Korán to him. Bernier, who disliked Aurangzíb, says that the indulgence and respect he showed to his captive father were exemplary. He consulted him like an oracle, and there was nothing he would not give him, except liberty. The two became partly reconciled, and the father bestowed his blessing and forgiveness on the son: but they never met. Sháh-Jahán died[1] at the beginning of 1666 at the age of

[1] There is no foundation for Mr. Talboys Wheeler's story of the Emperor's having been poisoned by Aurangzíb, except the insinuations of Catrou, whose evidence deserves little credit. It is incon-

seventy-six. The Emperor hastened to Agra to pay respect to his obsequies, and the body was laid in a tomb near the beautiful Táj, which the late sovereign had set up in memory of his wife.

The Princess Royal, who had shared his captivity with more than a daughter's devotion, was allowed to keep her state, in splendid seclusion, unmolested by the brother she had consistently opposed. 'She died with the fame of her past beauty still fresh, unmarried, at the age of sixty-seven. Her grave lies close to a saint's and to a poet's, in that *campo santo* of marble lattice work, near the Hall of the Sixty Four Pillars, beyond the Delhi walls. But only a piece of pure white marble, with a little grass piously watered, marks the Princess's grave. "Let no rich canopy surmount my resting-place," was her dying injunction, inscribed on the headstone. "This grass is the best covering for the grave of a lowly heart, the humble and transitory Ornament of the World, the disciple of the Holy Man of Chist, the daughter of the Emperor Sháh-Jahán [1].''' Her public memorials are the great rest-house for travellers at Delhi, and the splendid mosque of Agra.

The fate of the other princes must be told in few words. The day after Sháh-Jahán had been safely locked up, Aurangzíb, who had been in camp till now, entered Agra, occupied Dárá's house, seized his trea-

ceivable that the death should have been kept secret for more than a year, as Mr. Wheeler would have it; or that Aurangzíb should have waited six years to perpetrate so obvious a political execution.

[1] Sir W. W. Hunter, in 'Nineteenth Century,' May, 1887.

sure (amounting to 17 lacs of rupees), and the same day set out in pursuit of his fugitive brother. Murád-Bakhsh, who had all this time been enjoying the honours of kingship, and had revelled in the title of *Hazrat*, Your Majesty, which Aurangzíb lavished upon him, accompanied the latter in all the glory of mock sovereignty and twenty-six lacs of rupees in his money bags. They had not put many miles between their camp and Agra, when Aurangzíb connived in making his boorish brother disgracefully drunk, and, virtuously expressing his horror at the sight, and his conviction that so indiscreet a violator of the law of Islam could never be permitted to sit on the throne, threw him into chains (5th July). That night he was secretly conveyed to the state prison in the island fortress of Salímgarh, opposite Delhi. It needed all Aurangzíb's smooth eloquence and a lavish expenditure of bakhshísh to 'square' the army, who had all the soldier's respect for a brave officer and the seasoned trooper's toleration of a drunken man: but it was done, and the successful diplomatist led the combined forces in the footsteps of Dárá.

He went by forced marches, day and night, with his usual unflagging energy; lived the life of a common soldier; ate nothing but meal, drank bad water, and slept on the bare ground. His endurance of hardships awed his followers; but Dárá's own fatal tendency to political suicide saved his brother further trouble. The misguided prince, when aware of Aurangzíb's pursuit, instead of seeking to build up a formidable resistance at Kábul, where he was sure of the support of the governor, Mahábat Khán, turned south to Sind. Aurangzíb at once saw that the enemy had practically disarmed himself; and, leaving a few thousand horse to keep up the chase, he returned to the east, where Shujá' had again raised the standard of civil war. To sum up many months of misfortune, Dárá once more braved the army of Aurangzíb in the hills near Ajmír, and, after four days' hard fighting, was again put to flight. With his wife and daughter and a few servants he made for Ahmadábád. The servants plundered his baggage and ravished the jewels of the princesses, and, to crown his misery, when the fugitive at length reached the once friendly city, he found its gates closed against him. The Governor dared not risk his life in a hopeless cause.

'I had now been three days with Dárá,' says Bernier, 'whom I met on the road by the strangest chance imaginable; and, being destitute of any medical attendant, he compelled me to accompany him in the capacity of physician. . . . It was at break of day that the Governor's message was delivered, and the shrieks of the females drew tears from every eye. We were all overwhelmed with confusion and dismay, gazing in speechless horror at each other, at a loss what plan to recommend, and ignorant of the fate which perhaps awaited us from hour to hour. We observed Dárá stepping out, more dead than alive, speaking now to one, then to another; stopping and consulting even the commonest soldier. He saw consternation depicted in every countenance, and felt assured that he should be left without a single follower: but what was to become of him? Whither must he go? To delay his departure was to accelerate his ruin.'

So he took refuge among the robbers of Kachh. His wife died of hardship and misery, and he deprived himself of his scanty escort in order to send her body to be honourably interred at Lahore. His host, the Afghán Malik Jivan of Dhandar, seized the opportunity of his guest's defenceless condition, and carried him to Aurangzíb. Thus after few welcomes and many rejections, after bitter bereavement and weary wanderings, the Crown Prince and would-be Emperor of India was betrayed into the hands of his enemy. He was paraded through the streets of Delhi dressed in the meanest clothes, on a wretched elephant, covered with filth, and the tumult which this barbarous humiliation stirred up among the people nearly amounted to a rebellion. 'Everywhere,' says Bernier, 'I observed the people weeping and lamenting the fate of Dárá in the most touching language: men, women, and children wailing as if some mighty calamity had happened to themselves.' They went near to murdering the Afghán who had betrayed his guest, and showed such alarming sympathy with Dárá, that Aurangzíb resolved upon his speedy execution. He could not feel safe while his brother lived. A council was held, in which Raushan-Árá exerted all her eloquence against her unhappy brother; he was found to be an apostate and the ally of infidels; and on the 15th of September, 1659, he was ordered to execution. When he was dead his body was carried round the city to prove to all men that the deed was done, and 'many wept over his fate.' His head was taken to Aurangzíb, who had it carefully washed from blood, to make sure of its identity, and then ordered it to be buried in the tomb of Humáyún.

Shujá' gave more trouble than his elder brother. In response to Dárá's appeal he had again risen in arms in Bengal, (where he still held the position of Viceroy,) and even pushed his successes so far as to occupy Benáres and Alláhábád and annex Jaunpúr. Aurangzíb had turned from the pursuit of Dárá to meet this new danger, and he had an admirable lieutenant in Mír Jumla, who came from the Deccan to join his ancient ally. Together they defeated Shujá', in spite of the support he received from the Portuguese of Húglí, and the treachery of the Mahárája Jaswant Singh, who put the imperial camp in confusion by endeavouring to desert to his old friend Shujá' the night before the battle. Aurangzíb's coolness and Mír Jumla's strategy and valour won the day, and Prince 'Valiant' was hunted away to Arakán, whither he was conveyed by Portuguese pirates, who robbed whilst they saved him (1660). The last glimpse we get of him is tragical: wounded and insulted, he fled over the mountains, with but one woman and three faithful followers—and was heard of no more.

By this time there was not a rival in the field. Death or the dungeon had accounted for all other aspirants to the throne. The gloomy fortress of Gwáliór held Dárá's two sons, Sulaimán and Sipihr

Shukóh, and Aurangzíb's eldest son Muhammad, who in a rash moment had gone over to the side of his uncle Shujá', and repented of it in prison till he died in 1676. Murád-Bakhsh, who had also been removed there, attempted to escape, and was in consequence tried on an old count of murder and executed in December, 1661. Two daughters of Aurangzíb were given in marriage to the prisoners: one was allotted to the younger son of Dárá, and a similar consolation was awarded to the son of Murád-Bakhsh. It seemed that old sores did not rankle with these complaisant bridegrooms.

There remained no further obstacle in the path of Aurangzíb. He had already assumed the insignia of royalty. He had indeed first been hastily proclaimed Emperor in the garden of Shálimár outside Delhi, in the last days of July, 1658, without asserting the prerogatives of sovereignty, the coinage and public Prayer for the King. But on the 26th of May, 1659, he had formally ascended the throne in state.

CHAPTER III

THE PURITAN

WHEN Aurangzíb was for a second time proclaimed Emperor in May 1659, he took for his title the Persian word engraved on the sword which his captive father had given him—'Álamgír, 'World-compeller' —and by this title he was known to his subjects and to succeeding generations of Muslims. Before we consider the use he made of his power we must realize something of his character. All Muhammadan writers extol him as a saint; all contemporary Christians—except Dryden, and he was no historian, —denounce him as a hypocrite who used religion as a cloak for ambition, and said prayers to cover the most unnatural murders. Aurangzíb has experienced the fate of his great contemporary, Cromwell, whom he resembled in many features of the soul. He has had his Ludlow among his biographers, and his Baxter, with their theories of selfish ambition and virtue vitiated by success; he has also been slavered with the panegyrics of Muhammadan Flecknoes and Dawbeneys. These opposite views, however, are less contradictory than might be supposed.

They merely represent the difference between Christian bigotry and Muhammadan bigotry. To the Musalmán of India Aurangzíb is the ideal type of the devout and uncompromizing Muhammadan King, and his sanguinary advance to the throne is forgotten in his subsequent zeal for the faith and undeviating observance of the law and practice of Islám. On the other hand, Christian observers of the Great Mogul could not divest themselves of the western idea that a prince who says his prayers in public, like the Pharisee in the street, must necessarily be an ostentatious hypocrite; while they failed to reconcile the enormity of fratricide with piety or even common humanity. They did not understand the nature of the religion which could be honestly professed by such a man as Aurangzíb, any more than the royalists of the Restoration could discover in the ambitious regicide the sincere Christian that Cromwell really was.

The executions which paved the path of Aurangzíb to the throne lie at the root of the denunciations of his detractors. They forgot the proverb which Sultán Báyazíd used effectively in his negotiations with his brother, Prince Jem: 'Kingship counts no kinship.' They did not remember the repeated lessons of oriental history which taught Aurangzíb, and many before and after him, that a monarch's deadliest enemies are those of his own household. The 'Othmánlí Sultáns had long recognized the principle of political fratricide. Muhammad 'the Gentleman,' father of Murád the Great, humane as he was by nature, blinded his brother and slew his nephew. He had witnessed the disastrous effects of civil war among Ottoman scions, and he would not suffer the empire to be again plunged into the like intestine troubles. An oriental prince cannot be happy without a throne, and 'it becomes a matter of sheer necessity, and not a question of jealous suspicion, to make it impossible for him to attain his ambition. In the present day this is done by imprisoning him in the seraglio till he becomes idiotic. The old, and perhaps the more merciful way, was to kill him outright[1].'

Aurangzíb, in his heart, was at least as humanely disposed as the Gentleman Sultán of Turkey, but he had equal reason to dread the ambitious tempers of his brothers and kindred. His forefathers had suffered from the rebellions of their nearest relations. Akbar had to fight his brother; Jahángír rebelled against his father, and in turn was resisted by his own eldest son, who was condemned to pass his life in prison, where he was a perpetual anxiety to the government; Sháh-Jahán had defied his father, and came to the throne through the blood of his brother Shahriyár. With such warnings, Aurangzíb could expect no peace whilst Dárá, Shujá', and Murád-Bakhsh lived. Each of them had as good a right to the throne as he had himself, for there was no law of succession among Mughal princes; and each of them

[1] See my *History of Turkey* (1888), p. 83.

unmistakably intended to grasp the sceptre if he could. Aurangzíb might indeed have renounced the dream of power, and reverted to the ascetic ideal of his youth: but Dárá and Shujá' were infidels or heretics whom it was his duty, as a true Muslim, to drive from the throne; moreover, the lust of power was hot in his blood; besides, the Prince-Fakír would never have been safe from the knives of his brothers' agents. Death or imprisonment for life was the alternative fate of rival aspirants to the throne, and Aurangzíb chose to inflict the former. It was shocking, but safe, and on the whole more merciful: but to men of generous hearts it might have been impossible.

The shrewdest of all contemporary European witnesses, the French doctor Bernier, who was a spectator of the horrors of the fratricidal war, a sympathizer with Dárá, and no lenient critic of Aurangzíb, at whose court he spent eight observant years, sums up the whole matter with his usual fairness:

'My readers,' he says, 'have no doubt condemned the means by which the reigning Mughal attained the summit of power. These means were indeed unjust and cruel; but it is not perhaps fair to judge him by the rigid rules which we apply to the character of European princes. In our quarter of the globe, the succession to the crown is settled in favour of the eldest son by wise and fixed laws; but in Hindústán the right of governing is usually disputed by all the sons of the deceased monarch, each of whom is reduced to the cruel alternative of sacrificing his brothers that he himself may reign, or of suffering his own life to be forfeited for the security and stability of the dominion of another. Yet even those who may maintain that the circumstances of country, birth, and education afford no palliation of the conduct pursued by Aurangzíb, must admit that this Prince is endowed with a versatile and rare genius, that he is a consummate statesman, and a great King[1].'

The hostile criticisms of travellers regard chiefly Aurangzíb's conduct as Prince: to his acts as Emperor they manifest little save admiration. Throughout his long reign of nearly fifty years no single deed of cruelty has been proved against him[2]. Even his persecution of the Hindús, which was of a piece with his puritanical character, was admittedly marked by no executions or tortures. Hypocrite as he was called, no instance of his violating the precepts of the religion he professed has ever been produced, nor is there the smallest evidence that he ever forced his conscience. Like Cromwell, he may not have been 'a man scrupulous about words, or names, or such things,' but he undoubtedly 'put himself forth for the cause of God,' like the great Protector, 'a mean instrument to do God's people some good, and God service.'

Aurangzíb was, first and last, a stern Puritan. Nothing in life—neither throne, nor love, nor ease—weighed for an instant in his mind against his fealty

[1] Bernier, p. 199.

[2] The barbarous execution of Sambhájí is an exception, perhaps; but it was provoked by the outrageous virulence of the prisoner. Catrou's allegations of cruelty are merely general and supported by no individual instances, or by any evidence worthy the name.

to the principles of Islám. For religion he persecuted the Hindús and destroyed their temples, while he damaged his exchequer by abolishing the time-honoured tax on the religious festivals and fairs of the unbelievers. For religion's sake he waged his unending wars in the Deccan, not so much to stretch wider the boundaries of his great empire as to bring the lands of the heretical Shí'a within the dominion of orthodox Islám. To him the Deccan was *Dár-al-Harb*: he determined to make it *Dár-al-Islám*. Religion induced Aurangzíb to abjure the pleasures of the senses as completely as if he had indeed become the fakír he had once desired to be. No animal food passed his lips, and his drink was water; so that, as Tavernier says, he became 'thin and meagre, to which the great fasts which he keeps have contributed. During the whole of the duration of the comet [four weeks, in 1665], which appeared very large in India, where I then was, Aurangzíb only drank a little water and ate a small quantity of millet bread; this so much affected his health that he nearly died, for besides this he slept on the ground, with only a tiger's skin over him; and since that time he has never had perfect health[1].' Following the Prophet's precept that every Muslim should practise a trade, he devoted his leisure to making skull-caps, which were doubtless bought up by the courtiers of Delhi with the same enthusiasm as was shown by the ladies of Moscow for Count Tolstoi's boots. He not only knew the Korán by

[1] Tavernier's *Travels*, transl. Dr. V. Ball (1889), vol. i. p. 338.

heart, but copied it twice over in his fine calligraphy, and sent the manuscripts, richly adorned, as gifts to Mecca and Medína. Except the pilgrimage, which he dared not risk, lest he should come back to find an occupied throne, he left nothing undone of the whole duty of the Muslim. Even the English merchants of Súrat, who had their own reasons for disliking the Emperor, could only tell Ovington that Aurangzíb was 'a zealous professor' of Islám, 'never neglecting the hours of devotion nor anything which in his sense may denominate him a sincere believer[1].'

The native historians have nothing but praise to bestow upon Aurangzíb's character as a true Muslim. A contemporary historian, who lived some time at Court, and was a favourite with the Emperor, has recorded an elaborate description of the Great Mogul's religious practices[2], which is worth quoting. Its tone, fulsome as it appears, is not more adulatory than Bernier's letter to Colbert of the same period:—

'Be it known to the readers of this work that this humble slave of the Almighty is going to describe in a correct manner the excellent character, the worthy habits, and the refined morals of this most virtuous monarch, Abu-l-Muzaffar Muhyí ad dín Muhammad Aurangzíb 'Álamgír, according as he has witnessed them with his own eyes. The Emperor, a great worshipper of God by natural propensity, is remarkable for his rigid attachment to religion. He is a follower of the doctrines of the Imám Abú Hanífa (may God be pleased with him!) and establishes the five fundamental

[1] Ovington's *Voyage to Suratt in the year* 1689 (Lond. 1696), p. 195.
[2] *Mirát-i 'Álam*, Elliot and Dowson's *Hist. of India*, vol. vii. pp. 156–162.

doctrines of the *Kanz*. Having made his ablutions, he always occupies a great part of his time in adoration of the Deity, and says the usual prayers, first in the *masjid* [mosque] and then at home, both in congregation and in private, with the most heartfelt devotion. He keeps the appointed fasts on Fridays and other sacred days, and he reads the Friday prayers in the *jámi' masjid* [congregational mosque] with the common people of the Muhammadan faith. He keeps vigils during the whole of the sacred nights, and with the light of the favour of God illumines the lamps of religion and prosperity. From his great piety, he passes whole nights in the mosque which is in his palace, and keeps company with men of devotion. In privacy he never sits on a throne. He gave away in alms before his accession a portion of his allowance of lawful food and clothing, and now devotes to the same purpose the income of a few villages . . . and salt-producing tracts, which are appropriated to his privy purse. During the whole month of Ramazán he keeps fast, says the prayers appointed for that month, and reads the holy Korán in the assembly of religious and learned men, with whom he sits for that purpose during six and sometimes nine hours of the night. During the last ten days of the month he performs worship in the mosque; and, although on account of several obstacles he is unable to proceed on a pilgrimage to Mecca, yet the care which he takes to promote facilities for pilgrims to that holy place may be considered equivalent to the pilgrimage. . . .

'He never puts on the clothes prohibited by religion, nor does he ever use vessels of silver or gold[1]. In his sacred court no improper conversation, no word of backbiting or of falsehood is allowed. . . . He appears two or three times

[1] Nevertheless Tavernier (vol. i. p. 288) says he saw Aurangzíb drink out of a rock-crystal cup with a gold cover and saucer, enriched with diamonds, rubies, and emeralds.

every day in his Court of Audience with a pleasing countenance and mild look to dispense justice to complainants, who come in numbers without any hindrance; and as he listens to them with great attention, they make their representations without any fear or hesitation, and obtain redress from his impartiality. If any person talks too much or acts in an improper manner, he is never displeased, and he never knits his brows. His courtiers have often desired to prohibit people from showing so much boldness, but he remarks that by hearing their very words and seeing their gestures, he acquires a habit of forbearance and tolerance. . . . Under the dictates of anger and passion he never issues orders of death. . . .

'He is a very elegant writer in prose, and has acquired proficiency in versification; but agreeably to the words of God, *Poets deal in falsehoods*, he abstains from practising it. He does not like to hear verses except those which contain a moral. "To please Almighty God, he never turned his eye towards a flatterer, nor gave his ear to a poet."'

This is the character of a strict Muslim. The description is avowedly a panegyric, but nevertheless perfectly natural and probable in the judgment of every man who knows what the life of a really rigid Muslim is, such a life as a strict Wahhábí's. There is nothing in the portrait which is inconsistent with the whole tenour of Aurangzíb's career or with the testimony of European eyewitnesses. Exaggerated as it must seem to a western reader, the Indian historian's picture of his revered Emperor does not present a single touch which cannot be traced in the writings of contemporary French and English travellers, and in the statements of other native chroniclers who were less under the influence of the sitter for the portrait. Dr. Careri draws a precisely similar picture of the Emperor as he was in his old age in 1695. But the practice of such austerity as we see in this description is not the less remarkable because it is no more than what the religion of Islám exacts of the true believer. Aurangzíb might have cast the precepts of Muhammad to the winds and still kept—nay, strengthened—his hold of the sceptre of Hindústán. After the general slaughter of his rivals, his seat on the Peacock Throne was as secure as ever had been Sháh-Jahán's or Jahángír's. They held their power in spite of flagrant violations of the law of Islám; they abandoned themselves to voluptuous ease, to 'Wein, Weib, und Gesang,' and still their empire held together; even Akbar, model of Indian sovereigns, owed much of his success to his open disregard of the Muhammadan religion. The empire had been governed by men of the world, and thier government had been good. There was nothing but his own conscience to prevent Aurangzíb from adopting the eclectic philosophy of Akbar, the luxurious profligacy of Jahángír, or the splendid ease of Sháh-Jahán. The Hindús would have preferred anything to a Muhammadan bigot. The Rájput princes only wanted to be let alone. The Deccan would never have troubled Hindústán if Hindústán had not invaded it. Probably any other Mughal prince would have followed in the steps of the kings his forefathers, and emulated the indolence and vice of the Court in which he had received his earliest impressions.

Aurangzíb did none of these things. For the first time in their history the Mughals beheld a rigid Muslim in their Emperor—a Muslim as sternly repressive of himself as of the people around him, a king who was prepared to stake his throne for the sake of the faith. He must have known that compromise and conciliation formed the easiest and safest policy in an empire composed of heterogeneous elements of race and religion. He was no youthful enthusiast when he ascended the throne at Delhi, but a ripe man of forty, deeply experienced in the policies and prejudices of the various sections of his subjects. He must have been fully conscious of the dangerous path he was pursuing, and well aware that to run a-tilt against every Hindú sentiment, to alienate his Persian adherents, the flower of his general staff, by deliberate opposition to their cherished ideas, and to disgust his nobles by suppressing the luxury of a jovial court, was to invite revolution. Yet he chose this course, and adhered to it with unbending resolve through close on fifty years of unchallenged sovereignty. The flame of religious zeal blazed as hotly in his soul when he lay dying among the ruins of his Grand Army of the Deccan, an old man on the verge of ninety, as when, in the same fatal province, but then a youth in the springtime of life, he had thrown off the purple of viceregal state and adopted the mean garb of a mendicant fakír.

All this he did out of no profound scheme of policy, but from sheer conviction of right. Aurangzíb was born with an indomitable resolution. He had early formed his ideal of life, and every spring of his vigorous will was stretched at full tension in the effort to attain it. His was no ordinary courage. That he was physically brave is only to say he was a Mughal Prince of the old lion-hearted stock. But he was among the bravest even in their valiant rank. In the crisis of the campaign in Balkh, when the enemy 'like locusts and ants' hemmed him in on every side, and steel was clashing all around him, the setting sun heralded the hour of evening prayer: Aurangzíb, unmoved amid the din of battle, dismounted and bowed himself on the bare ground in the complicated ritual of Islám, as composedly as if he had been performing the *rik'a* in the mosque at Agra. The king of the Uzbegs noted the action, and exclaimed, 'To fight with such a man is self-destruction!' In the decisive battle with Dárá, when the fortune of the day seemed cast against him, and only a small band surrounded him, he revived the courage of his wavering troops by a simple but typical act: he ordered his elephant's legs to be chained together.

On his return towards Lahore from the pursuit of Dárá in Multán, pressing on with his customary forced marches, and riding ahead of his army, as usual, he was amazed to see the Rája Jai Singh, whom he believed to be at Delhi, advancing upon him at the head of 4000 or 5000 Rájputs. The Rája had been a loyal servant of Sháh-Jahán, and it was rumoured that he had hurried to Lahore with the design of seizing the usurper and restoring his old master to power. Aurangzíb knew he was in imminent peril, but he lost not a jot of his self-possession. 'Hail, my Lord Rája!' he cried, riding straight up to Jai Singh, 'Hail, my Lord Father! I have impatiently awaited you. The war is over, Dárá is ruined and wanders alone.' Then taking off his pearl necklace, and putting it round the Rájput's neck, he said, 'My army is weary, and I am fain that you should go to Lahore, lest it be in revolt. I appoint you Governor of the city and commit all things to your hands. We shall soon meet; I thank you for disposing of Sulaimán Shukóh. Haste to Lahore. *Salámat bachist*: farewell!' And Jai Singh obeyed. He did more—he persuaded his neighbour, Jaswant Singh of Márwár, to abandon the cause of Dárá and submit to Aurangzíb.

When stricken down with an agonizing malady the Emperor never lost sight of his duty. From his sick-bed he directed the affairs of his kingdom, and, as Bernier records, with the wonder of an experienced physician,

> 'On the fifth day of his illness, during the crisis of the disorder, he caused himself to be carried into the assembly of the Omrahs [or nobles[1]], for the purpose of undeceiving those who might believe he was dead, and of preventing a popular tumult or any accident by which Sháh-Jahán might effect his escape. The same reasons induced him to visit

[1] 'Omrah' is the usual form employed by the old travellers for Amír, of which the plural is Umará, whence 'Omrah.'

that assembly on the seventh, ninth, and tenth days; and, what appears almost incredible, on the thirteenth day, when scarcely recovered from a swoon so deep and long that his death was generally reported, he sent for the Rája Jai Singh and two or three of the principal Omrahs, for the purpose of verifying his existence. He then desired the attendants to raise him in the bed; called for paper and ink that he might write to Etbar-Khán, and despatched a messenger for the Great Seal. . . . I was present when my Ága became acquainted with all these particulars, and heard him exclaim, "What strength of mind! What invincible courage! Heaven reserve thee, Aurangzíb, for greater achievements! Thou art not yet destined to die[1].'"

Bernier's scholarly patron, Danishmand Khán, said no more than the truth. There is something greater than common courage in these actions. Nor was such contempt of danger and pain limited to his younger days. The old Emperor in his last campaigns in the Deccan shared the perils and hardships of the common soldier, and recklessly exposed himself to the enemy's sharpshooters[2].

Aurangzíb was not only brave in face of danger and in battling with bodily weakness: he had an invincible moral courage—the courage of the man who dares to act unflinchingly up to his convictions. He showed this in his dealings with the powerful but, to him, heretical sect of the Persian Shí'ís, who had been the backbone of Akbar's army and still formed the best tacticians on his staff. Akbar had adopted

[1] Bernier, pp. 125, 126.

[2] See below, pp. 195 196.

the solar year of the Persians, and had authorized the celebration of the Nauróz, or New Year's festival, a characteristic national institution of Persia. One of Aurangzíb's earliest acts after his accession was to prohibit the Nauróz and revert to the clumsy lunar reckoning of orthodox Muhammadanism. In vain did scholars and mathematicians point out the inconvenience of the lunar method, with its ever-shifting months, for the purposes of administration, collection of revenue, regulation of seasons, harvests, and a thousand other matters. All these things were patent to a man of Aurangzíb's shrewd intelligence; but they weighed nothing against the fact that the lunar system was the kalendar of Muhammad the Prophet, and whatever Muhammad the Prophet ordained should be law whilst Aurangzíb was king.

CHAPTER IV

The Emperor

In matters of religion the Emperor was obstinate to the point of fanaticism. In other matters he displayed the wisdom and judgment of a clear and thoughtful mind. As he had his ideal of faith, which he fought for *à outrance*, so had he his standard of kingly duty and his theory of the education of princes for the responsibilities of government.

'No man,' says Bernier, 'can be more alive than Aurangzíb to the necessity of storing the minds of princes, destined to rule nations, with useful knowledge. As they surpass others in power and elevation, so ought they, he says, to be pre-eminent in wisdom and virtue. He is very sensible that the cause of the misery which afflicts the empires of Asia, of their misrule, and consequent decay, should be sought, and will be found, in the deficient and pernicious mode of instructing the children of their kings. Entrusted from their infancy to the care of women and eunuchs, slaves from Russia, Circassia, Mingrelia, Georgia, or Ethiopia, whose minds are debased by the very nature of their occupation; servile and mean to superiors, proud and oppressive to dependents;—these princes, when called to the throne, leave the walls of the seraglio quite ignorant of the duties imposed upon them by their new situation. They appear on the stage of life as if they came from another world, or emerged for the first time from a subterraneous cavern, astonished, like simpletons, at all around them[1].'

Aurangzíb's notions of what the education of a prince should be are set forth in the reproof he administered to his old tutor when the latter hastened to Delhi in the hope of a handsome reward from his newly-crowned pupil. After taxing the venerable preceptor of his boyhood—who appears to have been an ordinary Muslim schoolmaster, such as may still be met with all over the East—with his ignorance of the geography and relative importance of European States, the Emperor went on thus:—

'Was it not incumbent upon my preceptor to make me acquainted with the distinguishing features of every nation of the earth; its resources and strength; its mode of warfare, its manners, religion, form of government, and wherein its interests principally consist; and, by a regular course of historical reading, to render me familiar with the origin of States; their progress and decline; the events, accidents, or errors, owing to which such great changes and mighty revolutions have been effected? . . . A familiarity with the language of surrounding nations may be indispensable in a king; but you would teach me to read and write Arabic; doubtless conceiving that you placed me under an everlasting obligation for sacrificing so large a portion of time to the study of a language wherein no one can hope to become proficient without ten or twelve years of close application. Forgetting how many important subjects ought to be embraced in the education of a prince, you acted as if it were chiefly necessary that he should possess great skill

[1] Bernier, pp. 144, 145.

in grammar, and such knowledge as belongs to a Doctor of Law; and thus did you waste the precious hours of my youth in the dry, unprofitable, and never-ending task of learning words! . . . Ought you not to have instructed me on one point at least, so essential to be known by a king, namely, on the reciprocal duties between the sovereign and his subjects? Ought you not also to have foreseen that I might at some future period be compelled to contend with my brothers, sword in hand, for the crown, and for my very existence? Such, as you must well know, has been the fate of the children of almost every king of Hindústán. Did you ever instruct me in the art of war, how to besiege a town, or draw up an army in battle array? Happy for me that I consulted wiser heads than thine on these subjects! Go! withdraw to thy village. Henceforth let no person know either who thou art or what is become of thee[1].'

The theory of royal education, thus expressed with some French periphrasis, would have done credit to Roger Ascham when he was training the vigorous intellect of the future Queen Elizabeth in her seclusion at Cheshunt. Aurangzíb's ideal of enlightened kingship is further expressed in a speech addressed to one of the most distinguished of the nobles, on the occasion of a remonstrance with the Emperor on his incessant application to affairs of State, which it was feared might endanger his health—and which very probably interfered with the licence and perquisites of the landed nobility.

'There can surely be but one opinion,' said the Emperor, 'among you wise men as to the obligation imposed upon

[1] Bernier, pp. 155-161.

a sovereign, in seasons of difficulty and danger, to hazard his life, and, if necessary, to die sword in hand in defence of the people committed to his care. And yet this good and considerate man would fain persuade me that the public weal ought to cause me no solicitude; that in devising means to promote it I should never pass a sleepless night, nor spare a single day from the pursuit of some low and sensual gratification. According to him, I am to be swayed by considerations of my own bodily health, and chiefly to study what may best minister to my personal ease and enjoyment. No doubt he would have me abandon the government of this vast kingdom to some vizier; he seems not to consider that, being born the son of a king and placed on the throne, I was sent into the world by Providence to live and labour, not for myself, but for others; that it is my duty not to think of my own happiness, except so far as it is inseparably connected with the happiness of my people. It is the repose and prosperity of my subjects that it behoves me to consult; nor are these to be sacrificed to anything besides the demands of justice, the maintenance of the royal authority, and the security of the State. This man cannot penetrate into the consequences of the inertness he recommends, and he is ignorant of the evils that attend upon delegated power. It was not without reason that our great Sa'dí emphatically exclaimed, "*Cease to be Kings! Oh, cease to be Kings! Or determine that your dominions shall be governed only by yourselves*[1]."'

This ideal of kingship accords with the tenour of the numerous letters which have been preserved from Aurangzíb's correspondence. In one of these, addressed to his captive father, he says:—

[1] Bernier, pp. 129 130.

'Almighty God bestows his trusts upon him who discharges the duty of cherishing his subjects and protecting the people. It is manifest and clear to the wise that a wolf is no fit shepherd, neither can a faint-hearted man carry out the great duty of government. Sovereignty is the guardianship of the people, not self-indulgence and profligacy. The Almighty will deliver your humble servant from all feeling of remorse as regards your Majesty [1].'

He made it absolutely clear to Sháh-Jahán that his usurping son would suffer no sentiment of filial piety to stand between him and his duty to the people:—

'I wish to avoid your censure,' he wrote in another letter to his father, 'and cannot endure that you should form a wrong estimate of my character. My elevation to the throne has not, as you imagine, filled me with insolence and pride. You know, by more than forty years' experience, how burthensome an ornament a crown is, and with how sad and aching an heart a monarch retires from the public gaze. . . . You seem to think that I ought to devote less time and attention to the consolidation and security of the kingdom, and that it would better become me to devise and execute plans of aggrandizement. I am indeed far from denying that conquests ought to distinguish the reign of a great monarch, and that I should disgrace the blood of the great Tímúr, our honoured progenitor, if I did not seek to extend the bounds of my present territories. At the same time, I cannot be reproached with inglorious inaction. . . . I wish you to recollect the greatest conquerors are not always the greatest kings. The nations of the earth have often been subjugated by mere uncivilised barbarians, and the most extensive con-

[1] Kháfi Khán, in Elliot and Dowson, vol. vii. p. 253.

quests have in a few short years crumbled to pieces. He is the truly great king who makes it the chief business of his life to govern his subjects with equity [1].'

One is naturally curious to trace how far Aurangzíb carried these admirable theories into practice—to discover whether he really tried to rule after the exalted standard he set up in his letters and conversation, or whether these were merely fine phrases and diplomatic assurances, such as the Emperor was only too fond of using. He was undoubtedly 'reserved, subtle, and a complete master of the art of dissimulation,' as Bernier says; and the utterances of a man so little frank, and so prone to the art of managing men by diplomatic craft rather than by an outspoken candour, require to be watched and weighed before they can be accepted as his honest convictions. All we know of his methods of government, however, goes to prove that his fine sentiments were really the ruling principles of his life. No act of injustice, according to the law of Islám, has been proved against him. Ovington, whose personal authority is worth little, but who derived his opinions and information from Aurangzíb's least partial critics, the English merchants at Bombay and Súrat, says that the Great Mogul is 'the main ocean of justice. . . . He generally determines with exact justice and equity; for there is no pleading of peerage or privilege before the Emperor, but the meanest man is as soon heard by Aurangzíb as the chief Omrah: which makes the

[1] Bernier, pp. 167, 168, who says he saw the letter.

Omrahs very circumspect of their actions and punctual in their payments[1].' The native chronicler, already quoted, has told us that the Emperor was a mild and painstaking judge, easy of approach, and gentle of manner; and the same character is given him by Dr. Careri, who saw him in the Deccan in 1695[2].

Generosity was not a salient virtue in the character of Aurangzíb, who was reputed to be avaricious and niggardly in matters of money and presents—though not in almsgiving: he could be generous to his poorer subjects. Soon after his accession to the throne he found that the late devastating movements of the contending armies, combined with a drought, had produced a famine in the land. He at once established houses for the distribution of free dinners, and ordered the remission of about eighty taxes, including the vexatious highway and ferry tolls, the ground cess on houses and shops, &c. Other taxes, such as those on Hindú and Muhammadan fairs, licences for spirits, gambling-hells, and houses of ill-fame, were probably abolished from religious motives: the Puritan King would not take toll for iniquity. But the rest could only have been remitted for the sake of helping a necessitous population. Aurangzíb had too strong an army at his back to be obliged to cultivate popularity at the cost of a serious loss to his exchequer. It is true the remission of many of these taxes was evaded by the local officials and landowners, who continued

[1] Ovington, p. 198. [2] See below, p. 198.

to collect them with the connivance of the imperial inspectors; but this was the fault of a defective or corrupt executive, not of the Emperor's good intention. When such infractions of his orders came to his knowledge the offenders were fined; but the royal anger was shortlived, and the culprits were too soon forgiven, and returned to their old ways of oppression. So mild, indeed, was the Emperor's rule that 'throughout the imperial dominions no fear and dread of punishment remained in the hearts' of the provincial and district officials, and the result was a state of administrative corruption and oppression worse than had ever been known under the paternal but watchful rule of Sháh-Jahán[1]. Cynical critics have explained Aurangzíb's ineffectual generosity as an ingenious contrivance to curry favour with the people without impoverishing the treasury. Dr. Careri seems to incline to the opinion that the Emperor connived at his Amírs' misdeeds in order to gain their support. A certain amount of conciliation of powerful chiefs, and even winking at their irregularities, is inseparable from a quasi-feudal administration, and Aurangzíb may have felt himself compelled sometimes to shut his eyes lest worse things should happen. The plain interpretation, however, of the remission of taxes as an act of bounty, dictated by the Koranic injunction of enevolence to 'the needy and the son of the road,' is simpler and more consistent with all we know of the Emperor's disposition. He was not the man

[1] Kháfí Khán, *l. c.*, vol. vii, pp. 246–8.

to connive at illegal extortion or the oppression of the poor; and his native Indian talents for craft and dissimulation, which aided him in his intrigues for the throne, and form a tradition in all Indian native government, were probably discounted by his fellow countrymen. Europeans are always apt to exaggerate the success of oriental guile, which may indeed deceive the plain man of the west, but is comparatively innocuous among brothers of the craft.

Indeed, Aurangzíb's habit of mind did not lend itself to trusting his officials and ministers overmuch, whether they were efficient or corrupt. As has been seen, he was no believer in delegated authority; and the lessons in treachery which the history of his dynasty afforded, and in which he had himself borne a part during the war of succession, sank deep into a mind naturally prone to suspicion. His father, Sháh-Jahán, said of him that, able as he was in war and in counsel, in action and administration, Aurangzíb 'was too full of subtle suspicion, and never likely to find anyone whom he could trust.' The prophecy came only too true. Aurangzíb never trusted a soul. That he lived in dread of poison is only what many Mughal princes endured: he had of course a taster—some say his daughter—to test the wholesomeness of his food, and if he took medicine his physician had to 'lead the way, take pill for pill, dose for dose,' that he might see their operation upon the body of the doctor before he ventured upon it himself[1]. His father had done

[1] Ovington, p. 209.

the like before him. Aurangzíb was served by a large staff of official reporters, called *Wáki' navís*, such as his forefathers—and for that matter the Khalifs of Baghdád, to quote high precedent—had also employed. These men, who were locally too well known to merit the opprobrious title of spies, sent regular letters from all the chief places in the provinces to keep the Great Mogul informed of all that went on in the most distant as well as the nearest districts. Their news-letters often brought information of the most important nature to the court; but they also communicated the most trifling events and conversations that came under the writers' notice. These correspondents were of course liable to be bribed by dishonest governors, and doubtless often suppressed what they should have reported; but they acted as a salutary check upon the local officials. They were, in fact, Crown inspectors, and were held in some dread by corrupt administrators and landowners. By their aid Aurangzíb was able to exercise his passion for business, to examine the minute details of administration, and to exercise his patronage down to the appointment of the merest clerk.

There was nothing new in this system of precaution: it was the usual oriental method. But he carried his check upon 'delegated authority' further than his predecessors. He adopted much the same plan as that which prevails in our own police system: he kept moving his officials about, and placed them as far as possible from their estates. In the words of Dr. Fryer, Aurangzíb

'governs by this maxim: To create as many Omrahs or nobles out of the Mughals or Persian followers as may be fairly entrusted, but always with this policy—To remove them to remote charges from that where their jágír or annuity arises; as not thinking it fit to trust them with forces or money in their allotted principalities, lest they should be tempted to unyoke themselves, and slip their neck from the servitude imposed upon them; for which purpose their wives and children are left as pledges at Court, while they follow the wars or are administering in cities and provinces; from whence, when they return, they have nothing they can call their own, only what they have cheated by false musters and a hard hand over both soldiers and people; which many times too, when manifest, they are forced to refund to the king, though not restore to the oppressed; for all money, as well as goods and lands, are properly his, if he call for them[1].'

This is a wider generalisation than is justified by the facts, and it appears from his letters that Aurangzíb repudiated the established Mughal custom of confiscating to the Crown the estates of deceased owners to the detriment of their natural heirs. But that he took every precaution that his ever alert suspicion could devise to paralyze the possible turbulence of his chief officers is true, and the growing family prestige of some of the great houses rendered it necessary. He carried his distrust to the point of nervous apprehension. He treated his sons as he treated his nobles, imprisoned his eldest for life, and kept his second

[1] Dr. John Fryer's *New Account of India* (Lond. 1698), p. 195.

son in captivity for six years upon a mere suspicion of disloyalty. It is true he had good reason to know the danger of a son's rebellion. His fourth son, Prince Akbar, joined the insurgent Rájputs against his father; and another, Prince A'zam, was always intriguing against the heir apparent, in a way that must have reminded Aurangzíb of his own treatment of Murád-Bakhsh. But, however well-founded in some cases, this general habit of distrust was fatal to the Emperor's popularity. Good Muslims of his own and later days have sung his praises and extolled his virtues; but the mass of his courtiers and officers lived in dread of arousing his suspicion, and, while they feared, resented his distrustful scrutiny. Aurangzíb was universally respected, but he was never loved. His father, Sháh-Jahán, in his graceful, indolent, selfish old age, even more than in his vigorous prime, was *pater patriae*, adored of his subjects. Aurangzíb was incomparably his father's superior—a wiser man, a juster king, a more clement and benevolent ruler; his greatest calumniator, Manucci, admits that his heart was really kind; yet all his self-restraint, his sense of duty, his equity, and laborious care of his people, counted for nothing in their hearts against his cold reserve and distrust. His very asceticism and economy and simplicity of life were repugnant to a nation accustomed to the splendour of Sháh-Jahán's magnificent court. The mass of his subjects felt that if they must have an alien in race and religion for their king, at least let him show himself a king right royally, and shed his sovereign radiance on his subjects, even while he emptied their purses upon his stately pleasures. This was just what Aurangzíb could not do. The very loftiness of his nature kept his people at a distance, while his inflexible uprightness and frigid virtue chilled their hearts.

This cold austerity of Aurangzíb destroyed his influence. Few kings have had better intentions, but the best will in the world will not bring popularity, or make men do what you think right merely because they know you think it so. The people saw through the suave manner and placid amiability of the judge who listened so indulgently to their petitions, and perceived a bigot's atrophied heart behind the gracious smile. It has been usual to call the character of Aurangzíb a puzzling compound of contradictions. Yet there is no inconsistency in his acts or words. His character is that of the Puritan, with all its fiery zeal, its ascetic restraint, its self-denial, its uncompromising tenacity of righteous purpose, its high ideals of conduct and of duty; and also with its cold severity, its curbed impulses, its fanaticism, its morbid distrust of 'poor human nature,' its essential unlovableness. Aurangzíb possessed many great qualities, he practised all the virtues; but he was lacking in the one thing needful in a leader of men: he could not win love. Such a one may administer an empire, but he cannot rule the hearts of men.

CHAPTER V

THE COURT [1]

SIMPLE of life and ascetic as he was by disposition, Aurangzíb could not altogether do away with the pomp and ceremony of a Court which had attained the pinnacle of splendour under his magnificent father. In private life it was possible to observe the rigid rules, and practise the privations of a saint; but in public the Emperor must conform to the precedents set by his royal ancestors from the days of Akbar, and hold his state with all the imposing majesty which had been so dear to Sháh-Jahán. Little as he was himself disposed to cultivate 'the pomps and vanities of this wicked world,' he was perfectly aware of their importance in the eyes of his subjects. A Great Mogul, without gorgeous darbárs, dazzling jewels, a glittering assemblage of armed and richly habited courtiers, and all the pageantry of royal state, would have been inconceivable, or contemptible,

[1] The prime authority on Aurangzíb's Court at Delhi is Bernier's *Travels*. His admirable description, full of the graphic power of an observant eye-witness, has been excellently rendered by Mr. Archibald Constable in his translation (*Constable's Oriental Miscellany*, vol. i. 1891), which I have been permitted to quote.

to a people who had been accustomed for centuries to worship and delight in the glorious spectacle of august monarchs enthroned amid a blaze of splendour. With Orientals, more even than with Europeans, the clothes make the king; and not his own subjects only, but the ambassadors of foreign Powers would have thought meanly of the Emperor if he had wholly cast off the purple and fine linen of his rank and neglected to receive them sumptuously, as became a *grand monarque.* Accordingly Aurangzíb followed, at least in his earlier years and in the more essential ceremonial details, the Court custom which had been handed down unchanged from the first organizer of the Empire, his great-grandfather Akbar.

The Emperor divided his residence between Delhi and Agra, but Delhi was the chief capital, where most of the state ceremonies took place. Delhi was the creation of the Mughals, for the old city of former kings had been dismantled and neglected to form the new capital of Sháh-Jahán-ábád, 'The City of Sháh-Jahán,' which that Emperor built in 1638–48, and, *more Mongolico*, named after himself. Agra had been the metropolis of Akbar, and usually of Jahángír; but its sultry climate interfered with the enjoyment of their luxurious successor, and the Court was accordingly removed, at least for a large part of the year, to New Delhi, the 'City of Sháh-Jahán.' The ruins of this splendid capital, its mosques, and the noble remains of its superb palace are familiar to every reader. To see it as it was in its glory, however, we must look through the eyes of Bernier, who saw it when only eleven years had passed since its completion. His description was written at the capital itself, in 1663, after he had spent four years of continuous residence there; so it may be assumed that he knew his Delhi thoroughly. The city, he tells us, was built in the form of a crescent on the right bank of the Jamna, which formed its north-eastern boundary, and was crossed by a single bridge of boats. The flat surrounding country was then, as now, richly wooded and cultivated, and the city was famous for its luxuriant gardens. Its circuit, save on the river side, was bounded by brick walls, without moat or fosse, and of little value for the purpose of defence, since they were scarcely fortified, save by some 'flanking towns of antique shape at intervals of about one hundred paces, and a bank of earth forming a platform behind the walls, four or five feet in thickness.' The circuit of the walls was six or seven miles; but outside the gates were extensive suburbs, where the chief nobles and wealthy merchants had their luxurious houses; and there also were the decayed and straggling remains of the older city just without the walls of its supplanter. Numberless narrow streets intersected this wide area, and displayed every variety of building, from the thatched mud and bamboo huts of the troopers and camp-followers, and the clay or brick houses of the smaller officials and merchants, to the spacious mansions of the chief nobles, with their courtyards and gardens, fountains and cool matted chambers, open to the four winds, where the afternoon siesta might be enjoyed during the heats.

Two main streets, perhaps thirty paces wide, and very long and straight, lined with covered arcades of shops, led into the 'great royal square' which fronted the fortress or palace of the Emperor. This square was the meeting-place of the citizens and the army, and the scene of varied spectacles. Here the Rájput Rájas pitched their tents when it was their duty to mount guard; for Rájputs never consented to be cooped up within Mughal walls. Here might be seen the cavalcade of the great nobles when their turn to watch arrived.

'Nothing can be conceived much more brilliant than the great square in front of the fortress at the hours when the Omrahs, Rájas, and Mansabdárs repair to the citadel to mount guard or attend the assembly of the Am-Khas [or Hall of Audience]. The Mansabdárs flock thither from all parts, well mounted and equipped, and splendidly accompanied by four servants, two behind and two before, to clear the street for their masters. Omrahs and Rájas ride thither, some on horseback, some on majestic elephants; but the greater part are conveyed on the shoulders of six men, in rich palankins, leaning against a thick cushion of brocade, and chewing their betel, for the double purpose of sweetening their breath and reddening their lips. On the one side of every palankin is seen a servant bearing the *pîkdan*, or spittoon of porcelain or silver; on the other side two more servants fan the luxurious lord, and flap away the flies, or brush off the dust with a peacock's-tail fan; three or four footmen march in front to clear the way, and a chosen number of the best formed and best mounted horsemen follow in the rear.

'Here too is held a bazar or market for an endless variety of things; which, like the Pont Neuf at Paris, is the rendezvous for all sorts of mountebanks and jugglers. Hither likewise the astrologers resort, both Muhammadan and Gentile [Hindú]. These wise doctors remain seated in the sun, on a dusty piece of carpet, handling some old mathematical instruments, and having open before them a large book which represents the signs of the zodiac. . . . They tell a poor person his fortune for a *páisa* (which is worth about one *sol*); and after examining the hand and face of the applicant, turning over the leaves of the large book, and pretending to make certain calculations, these impostors decide upon the *sá'at* or propitious moment of commencing the business he may have in hand.'

Among the rest a half-caste Portuguese from Goa sat gravely on his carpet, with an old mariner's compass and a couple of breviaries for stock in trade: he could not read them, it is true, but the pictures in them answered the turn, and he told fortunes as well as the best. *A tal Bestias, tal Astrologuo*, he unblushingly observed to the Jesuit Father Buzée, who saw him at his work. Nothing was done in India in those days without consulting astrologers, of whom these bazar humbugs were the lowest rank. Kings and nobles granted large salaries to these crafty diviners, and never undertook the smallest affair without taking their advice. 'They read whatever is written in heaven; fix upon the *sá'at*, and solve any doubt by opening the Korán.'

Beyond the 'great royal square' was the fortress, which contained the Emperor's palace and *mahall* or seraglio, and commanded a view of the river across the sandy tract where the elephant fights took place and the Rája's troops paraded. The lofty walls were slightly fortified with battlements and towers and surrounded by a moat, and small field pieces were pointed upon the town from the embrasures. The palace within was the most magnificent building of its kind in the East, and the private rooms or *mahall* alone covered more than twice the space of the Escurial or of any European palace. One entered the fort between two gigantic stone elephants carrying the statues of Rájas Jai Mal and Pattá of Chitór, who offered a determined resistance to Akbar, and, sooner than submit, died in a last desperate sally; so that their memory was cherished even by their enemies. Passing between these stone heroes 'with indiscribable awe and respect,' and crossing the courtyard within, the long and spacious Silver Street stretched before one, with its canal running down the middle, and its raised pavements and arcades on either side. Other streets opened in every direction, and here and there were seen the merchants' caravanserais and the great workshops where the artisans employed by the Emperor and the nobles plied their hereditary crafts of embroidery, silver and gold smithery, gun-making, lacquer-work, muslin, painting, turning, and so forth.

Delhi was famous for its skill in the arts and crafts. It was only under royal or aristocratic patronage that the artist flourished; elsewhere the artisan was at the mercy of his temporary employer, who paid him as he chose. The Mughal Emperors displayed a laudable appreciation of the fine arts, which they employed with lavish hands in the decoration of their palaces.

'The arts in the Indies,' says Bernier, 'would long ago have lost their beauty and delicacy, if the Monarch and principal Omrahs did not keep in their pay a number of artists who work in their houses.' Yet there 'are ingenious men in every part of the Indies. Numerous are the instances of handsome pieces of workmanship made by persons destitute of tools, and who can scarcely be said to have received instruction from a master. Sometimes they imitate [alas !] so perfectly articles of European manufacture, that the difference between the original and the copy could hardly be discerned. Among other things the Indians make excellent muskets and fowling-pieces, and such beautiful gold ornaments that it may be doubted if the exquisite workmanship of those articles can be exceeded by any European goldsmith. I have often admired the beauty, softness, and delicacy of their paintings and miniatures, and was particularly struck with the exploits of Akbar, painted on a shield, by a celebrated artist, who is said to have been seven years in completing the picture. The Indian painters are chiefly deficient in just proportions, and in the expression of the face.'

The orthodox Muhammadan objection to the representation of living things had been overruled by Akbar, who is recorded to have expressed his views on painting in these words :—

'There are many that hate painting; but such men I dislike. It appears to me as if a painter had quite peculiar means of recognizing God. For a painter in sketching anything that has life, and in devising its limbs one after the other, must come to feel that he cannot bestow individuality upon his work, and is thus forced to think of God, the giver of life, and will thus increase in knowledge.'

A large number of exquisite miniatures, or paintings on paper designed to illustrate manuscripts, or to form royal portrait-albums, have come down to us from the sixteenth and seventeenth centuries, which fully bear out Bernier's praise. The technique and detail are admirable, and the colouring and lights often astonishingly skilful. They include portraits of the emperors, princes, and chief nobles, which, in spite of Bernier's criticism, display unusual power in the delineation of individual countenances; and there are landscapes which are happily conceived and brilliantly executed[1]. There is no doubt that the Jesuit missions at Agra and other cities of Hindústán brought western ideas to bear upon the development of Indian painting. Jahángír, who was, by his own account, 'very fond of pictures and an excellent judge of them,' is recorded to have had a picture of the Madonna behind

[1] Mr. Archibald Constable has brought two of these interesting relics of a little-known art within the reach of all by reproducing them with marked success in his *Oriental Miscellany*, where the frontispiece to Bernier's *Travels* is a fine portrait of Sháh-Jahán, and a landscape of Akbar hunting by night illustrates Somervile's *Chace*, appended to Dryden's *Aureng-Zebe*. Both are after originals in Colonel H. B. Hanna's collection. The portrait of Aurangzíb prefixed to this volume is after a drawing by an Indian artist, contained in an album in the British Museum (Add. 18,801, no. 34), which bears the seal of Ashraf Khán and the date A. H. 1072 (1661, 2). It represents Aurangzíb at about the time of his accession, or perhaps somewhat earlier, and belongs to the rarest and finest class of Indian portraits.

a curtain, and this picture is represented in a contemporary painting which has fortunately been preserved[1]. Tavernier saw on a gate outside Agra a representation of Jahángír's tomb 'carved with a great black pall with many torches of white wax, and two Jesuit Fathers at the end,' and adds that Sháh-Jahán allowed this to remain because 'his father and himself had learnt from the Jesuits some principles of mathematics and astrology[2].' The Augustinian friar Manrique, who came to inspect the Jesuit missions, in the time of Sháh-Jahán, found the Prime-minister Ásaf Khán, at Lahore, in a palace decorated with pictures of Christian saints[3]. In most Mughal portraits, the head of the Emperor is surrounded by an aureole or nimbus, and many other features in the schools of painting at Agra and Delhi remind one of contemporary Italian art. The artists were held in high favour at Court, and many of their names have been preserved. Their works added notably to the decoration of the splendid and elaborate palaces which are amongst the most durable memorials of the Mughal period.

Leaving the artists' workshops, and traversing the guard's quadrangle, one reached the cynosure of all courtiers' eyes, the Hall of Audience, or Am-Khas; a vast court, surrounded by covered arcades, with a great open hall or sublimated portico, raised above

[1] In the collection of Colonel H. B. Hanna.

[2] *Travels*, vol. i. p. 111.

[3] Manrique, *Itinerario* (1649), p. 374.

the ground, on the further side, opposite the great gate. The roof of this hall was supported by rows of columns, and beautifully painted and gilt, and in the wall which formed its back was, and still is, the famous *jharukhá*,—the ample open window where the Great Mogul daily sat upon his throne to be seen of all the people who thronged the spacious court. On his right and left stood the Princes of the Blood; and beneath, in the hall itself, within a silver railing, were grouped the four Secretaries of State, and the chief nobles and officers of the realm, the Rájas, and the many ambassadors who came from foreign States, all standing with eyes cast to the ground and hands crossed in the customary attitude of respect, while the King's musicians discoursed 'sweet and pleasant music.' Further off, and lower down, outside the silver rail, the array of Mansabdárs and lesser nobles and officials gleamed with colour and jewels and steel, while the rest of the hall and the whole court were thronged with every class of the subjects, high and low, rich and poor, all of whom had the right to see and have audience of the Emperor. Once there, however, no one might leave the Presence until the levee was over.

The scene on any State occasion was imposing, and almost justified the inscription on the gateway: 'If there be a Heaven upon earth, it is Here, it is Here.' The approach of Aurangzíb was heralded by the shrill piping of the hautboys and clashing of cymbals from the band-gallery over the great gate:—

'The King appeared seated upon his throne at the end of the great hall in the most magnificent attire. His vest was of white and delicately flowered satin, with a silk and gold embroidery of the finest texture. The turban of gold cloth had an aigrette whose base was composed of diamonds of an extraordinary size and value, besides an oriental topaz which may be pronounced unparalleled, exhibiting a lustre like the sun. A necklace of immense pearls suspended from his neck reached to the stomach. The throne was supported by six massy feet, said to be of solid gold, sprinkled over with rubies, emeralds, and diamonds. It was constructed by Sháh-Jahán for the purpose of displaying the immense quantity of precious stones accumulated successively in the Treasury from the spoils of ancient Rájas and Pátáns, and the annual presents to the monarch which every Omrah is bound to make on certain festivals[1]. At the foot of the throne were assembled all the Omrahs, in splendid apparel, upon a platform surrounded by a silver railing and covered by a spacious canopy of brocade with deep fringes of gold. The pillars of the hall were hung with brocades of a gold ground, and flowered satin canopies were raised over the whole expanse of the extensive apartment, fastened with red silken

[1] Tavernier (i. 381–5) has recorded an elaborate description of the famous Peacock Throne, which resembled, he says, a bed, standing upon four (not six) massive feet, about two feet high, and was covered by a canopy supported by twelve columns, belted with fine pearls, from which hung the royal sword, mace, shield, bow and arrows. The throne was plated with gold and inlaid with diamonds, emeralds, pearls, and rubies. Above the canopy was a golden peacock with spread tail, composed of sapphires and other stones. On either side of the peacock were bouquets of golden flowers inlaid with precious stones; and in front were the parasols of state, fringed with pearls, which none but the Emperor was permitted to use. The throne is now preserved in the Shah's palace at Tihrán, and is valued at about £2,600,000. Bernier and Tavernier priced it much higher.

cords from which were suspended large tassels of silk and gold. The floor was covered entirely with carpets of the richest silk, of immense length and breadth. A tent, called the *aspek*, was pitched outside [in the court], larger than the hall, to which it joined by the top. It spread over half the court, and was completely enclosed by a great balustrade, covered with plates of silver. Its supporters were pillars overlaid with silver, three of which were as thick and as high as the mast of a barque, the others smaller. The outside of this magnificent tent was red, and the inside lined with elegant Masulipatan chintzes, figured expressly for that very purpose with flowers so natural and colours so vivid that the tent seemed to be encompassed with real parterres.

'As to the arcade galleries round the court, every Omrah had received orders to decorate one of them at his own expense, and there appeared a spirit of emulation who should best acquit himself to the Monarch's satisfaction. Consequently all the arcades and galleries were covered from top to bottom with brocade, and the pavement with rich carpets.'

The scene described so minutely by Bernier was exceptionally brilliant, and the reason assigned for the unusual splendour and extravagance of the decorations was Aurangzíb's benevolent desire to afford the merchants an opportunity for disposing of the large stock of brocades and satins which had been accumulating in their warehouses during the unprofitable years of the war of succession. But festivals of similar though less magnificence were held every year, on certain anniversaries, of which the chief was the Emperor's birthday, when, in accordance with time-honoured precedent, he was solemnly weighed in a pair of gold scales against precious metals and stones and food, all which was ostensibly to be distributed to the poor on the following day; and when the nobles one and all came forward with handsome birthday presents of jewels and golden vessels and coins, sometimes amounting altogether to the value of £2,000,000. On these occasions the fairest ladies of the chief nobles sometimes held a sort of fancy bazar in the imperial seraglio, where they sold turbans worked on cloth of gold, brocades, and embroideries to the Emperor and his wives and princesses at exorbitant prices, governed chiefly by the wit and beauty of the seller. A vast deal of good-humoured banter and haggling went on over these bargainings, and many a young lady made a reputation which served her in good stead when it came to the question of marrying her to a Court favourite. Of course no man but the Emperor was allowed to see these unveiled beauties, but the Mughal and his Begams were excellent match-makers, and could be trusted to do the best for the débutantes. The festivals generally ended with an elephant-fight, which was as popular in India as a bull-fight in Spain. Two elephants charged each other over an earth wall, which they soon demolished; their skulls met with a tremendous shock, and tusks and trunks were vigorously plied, till at length one was overcome by the other, when the victor was separated from his prostrate adversary by an explosion of fireworks between them. The chief sufferers were the mahouts or riders, who were frequently trodden under foot and killed on the spot; insomuch that they always took formal leave of their families before mounting for the hazardous encounter. In spite of their growing effeminacy, there was enough of the old savage Mughal blood in Aurangzíb's courtiers to make them delight in these dangerous and cruel exhibitions. Indeed, most of the spectac'es that enlivened the Court were of a warlike character; and luxurious as were their habits, the petticoated Mughals could still be roused to valour, while no nation produced keener sportsmen.

In the jovial days of Jahángír and Sháh-Jahán, the blooming Kenchens or Nautch girls used to play a prominent part in the Court festivities, and would keep the jolly emperors awake half the night with their voluptuous dances and agile antics. But Aurangzíb was 'unco gude' and would as soon tolerate idolatry as a Nautch. He did his best to suppress music and dancing altogether, in accordance with the example of the Blessed Prophet, who was born without an ear for music and therefore hastily ascribed the invention of harmony to the Devil. The musicians of India were certainly noted for a manner of life which ill accorded with Aurangzíb's strict ideas, and their concerts were not celebrated for sobriety. The Emperor determined to destroy them, and a severe edict was issued. Raids of the police dissipated their harmonious meetings, and their instruments were burnt. One Friday, as

Aurangzíb was going to the mosque, he saw an immense crowd of singers following a bier, and rending the air with their cries and lamentations. They seemed to be burying some great prince. The Emperor sent to inquire the cause of the demonstration, and was told it was the funeral of Music, slain by his orders, and wept by her children. 'I approve their piety,' said Aurangzíb gravely: 'let her be buried deep, and never be heard again[1].' Of course the concerts went on in the palaces of the nobles, but they were never heard at Court. The Emperor seriously endeavoured to convince the musicians of the error of their ways, and those who reformed were honoured with pensions.

Even on every day occasions, when there were no festivals in progress, the Hall of Audience presented an animated appearance. Not a day passed, but the Emperor held his levee from the jharukhá window, whilst the bevy of nobles stood beneath, and the common crowd surged in the court to lay their grievances and suits before the imperial judge. The ordinary levee lasted a couple of hours, and during this time the royal stud was brought from the stables opening out of the court, and passed in review before the Emperor, so many each day; and the household elephants, washed and painted black, with two red streaks on their foreheads, came in their embroidered caparisons and silver chains and bells, to be inspected

[1] Kháfí Khán, in Elliot and Dowson, vol. vii. pp. 283–4; Catrou, *Histoire générale de l'Empire du Mogol*, Troisième Partie (1715), p. 5.

by their master, and at the prick and voice of their riders saluted the Emperor with their trunks and trumpeted their *taslím* or homage. Hounds and hawks, hunting leopards, rhinoceroses, buffaloes, and fighting antelopes were brought forward in their turn; swords were tested on dead sheep; and the nobles' troops were paraded.

'But all these things are so many interludes to more serious matters. The King not only reviews his cavalry with particular attention, but there is not, since the war has been ended, a single trooper or other soldier whom he has not inspected and made himself personally acquainted with, increasing or reducing the pay of some, and dismissing others from the service. All the petitions held up in the crowd assembled in the Am-Khás are brought to the King and read in his hearing; and the persons concerned being ordered to approach are examined by the Monarch himself, who often redresses on the spot the wrongs of the aggrieved party. On another day of the week he devotes two hours to hear in private the petitions of ten persons selected from the lower orders, and presented to the King by a good and rich old man. Nor does he fail to attend the justice chamber on another day of the week, attended by the two principal Kázís or chief justices. It is evident, therefore, that barbarous as we are apt to consider the sovereigns of Asia, they are not always unmindful of the justice that is due to their subjects[1].'

The levee in the beautiful Audience Hall was not the Emperor's only reception in the day. In the evening he required the presence of every noble in the Ghuzl-Khána, a smaller and more private hall behind

[1] Bernier, p. 263.

the Am-Khas, but no less beautifully decorated. Here he would sit, surrounded by his Court, and 'grant private audiences to his officers, receive their reports, and deliberate on important matters of state.' This later reception was almost as ceremonious as the earlier one, but there was no space for reviews of cavalry: only the officers who had the honour to form the guard paraded before the Emperor, preceded by the insignia of royalty, the silver fish, dragon, lion, hands, and scales, emblematic of the various functions of sovereignty.

Close to the Hall of Audience was the imperial mosque, with its gilded dome, where Aurangzíb daily conducted the prayers. On Fridays he went in state to the Jámi' Masjid, the beautiful mosque which Sháh-Jahán completed just before his deposition. It stands on a rocky platform in the centre of Delhi, in a great square where four streets meet. The roads were watered before the procession passed, and soldiers kept the way. An advance guard of cavalry announced the approach of Aurangzíb, and presently the Emperor appeared, riding beneath a canopy on a richly caparisoned elephant, or seated upon a dazzling throne borne by eight men upon a gorgeous litter, while the nobles and officers of the Court and mace-bearers followed on horseback or in palankins.

'If we take a review,' concludes Bernier, 'of this metropolis of the Indies, and observe its vast extent and its numberless shops; if we recollect that, besides the Omrahs, the city never contains less than 35,000 troopers, nearly all of whom have wives, children, and a great number of servants, who, as well as their masters, reside in separate houses; that there is no house, by whomsoever inhabited, which does not swarm with women and children; that during the hours when the abatement of the heat permits the inhabitants to walk abroad, the streets are crowded with people, although many of those streets are very wide, and, excepting a few carts, unencumbered with wheel carriages; we shall hesitate before we give a positive opinion in regard to the comparative population of Paris and Delhi; and I conclude, that if the number of souls be not as large in the latter city as in our own capital, it cannot be greatly less.'

CHAPTER VI

The Government

No 'Turk'—to use the term of the old travellers—was ever brought into more difficult and delicate relations with 'infidels and heretics' than the Great Mogul. The Grand Signior at Constantinople had his own troubles in this same seventeenth century with his Christian subjects in Hungary and Greece. But Aurangzíb had to govern a people of whom at least three-fourths were what he termed infidels, and he had to govern them with the aid of officers who were no better than heretics to an orthodox Sunní. The vast majority of his subjects were Hindús; the best of his father's governors and generals had been Persians of the sect of the Shí'a; and Aurangzíb, in spite of his prejudices, found he could not do without those tried officials, if he was to make head against the leaders of the Hindús. The downtrodden peasantry could never give him serious trouble, indeed; but the Hindú Chiefs, the innumerable Rájas of the Ráj-put blood, dwelling in their mountain fastnesses about the Aravalli range and the Great Desert of India, were a perpetual source of danger to the throne. There were more than a hundred of these native princes, some of whom could bring at least 20,000 horsemen into action; and far from being the 'mild Hindús' of the plains, they were born fighters, the bravest of the brave, urged to fury by a keenly sensitive feeling of honour and pride of birth, and always ready to conquer or die for their chiefs and their privileges. To see the Rájputs rush into battle, maddened with *bang* and stained with orange turmeric, and throw themselves recklessly upon the enemy in a forlorn hope, was a spectacle never to be forgotten. Had their Rájas combined their forces, it is probable that no Mughal army could have long stood against them. Happily for the empire they were weakened by internal jealousies, of which Aurangzíb was not slow to take advantage. They could be played off, one against the other. Moreover, the wise conciliation of Akbar, following upon his triumphs in war, had done much to win the Rájput leaders over to the side of the invaders. There are few more instructive lessons in Indian history than the loyal response which the Hindú Chiefs made to the conciliating policy of Akbar. It was a Hindú, Todar Mal, who reduced Bengal to the imperial sceptre, and then organized the financial administration of the empire. Hindú generals and Bráhman poets led Akbar's armies, and governed some of his greatest provinces. Hindú clerks formed the chief official class in all departments where education was essential, and Rájput clans furnished the thews and sinews of his armies. Every Mughal Emperor, even the orthodox Aurangzíb, had carried on Akbar's policy of marrying Rájput princesses, and seeking them as wives for his sons. It was a distinct loss of caste to the queens, and the Rájput pride kicked sorely at it; but there were counter-balancing advantages in such alliances, and they undoubtedly tended to bind the Native Chiefs to the Mughal throne.

What with Rájputs, Pátáns, and Persians, to say nothing of the parties in the Deccan, Aurangzíb had a difficult population to deal with; and his first object, in self-defence, was to maintain a sufficient standing army to overawe each separate source of insurrection. He could indeed rely upon the friendly Rájas to take the field with their gallant followers against a Shí'ite kingdom in the Deccan, or in Afghánistán, and even against their fellow Rájputs. when the imperial cause happened to coincide with their private feuds. He could trust his Persian officers in a conflict with Pátáns or Hindús, though never against their Shí'ite coreligionists in the Deccan. But he needed a force devoted to himself alone, a body of retainers who looked to him for rank and wealth, and even the bare means of subsistence. This he found in the species of feudal system which had been inaugurated by Akbar. Just as the early 'Abbásid Khalifs had found safety and a sound imperial organization by selecting their provincial governors, not from the arrogant chiefs of the Arab clans, but from among their own freedmen, people of no family, who owed everything to their lord, and were devoted to his interests: so the Mughal Emperors endeavoured to bind to their personal interest a body of adventurers of any sort of origin, generally of low descent, perhaps formerly slaves, and certainly uneducated, who derived their power and affluence solely from their sovereign, who 'raised them to dignity or degraded them to obscurity according to his own pleasure and caprice.' This body was called *Mansabdárs*, or grant-holders, because each member received an income in money or land from the emperor. The *jágír* or estate of the mansabdár was the Mughal equivalent of the *timar* of the Ottoman timariots, and the feof of the Egyptian Mamlúk. The value of the *mansab*, or grant, whether paid in cash or lands, was carefully graduated; so that there were a series of ranks among the grantees corresponding to the degrees of *chin* in the Russian bureaucracy. The ranks were distinguished in accordance with the number of horse a mansabdár was supposed to maintain: and we read of mansabdárs of 500, or 1000, or 5000, and even 12000 horse. The higher ranks, from 1000 horse upwards, received the title of Amír, of which the plural is Umará. The writings of European travellers are full of references to these 'Omrahs,' or nobles, as they call them,—though it must not be forgotten that the nobility was purely official, and had no necessary connexion with birth or hereditary estates. The term an 'Amír of 5000,' however, did not imply a following of 5000 horsemen, though it doubtless meant this originally. It was merely a title of rank, and the number of cavalry that each Amír was bound to maintain was regulated by the King himself. An Amír of 5000 sometimes was ordered to keep only 500 horses; the rest was on paper only. As a matter of fact, he often kept much fewer than he was paid for; and what with false returns of his efficient force, and stopping part of the men's pay, the grantee enjoyed a large income. Yet the heavy expenses of the Court, the extravagance and enormous establishments of the Amírs, and the ruinous presents they were forced to make to the Emperor at the annual festivals, exhausted their resources, and involved them deeply in debt. In Bernier's time there were always twenty-five or thirty of these higher Amírs at the Court, drawing salaries estimated at the rate of from one to twelve thousand horse. The number in the provinces is not stated, but must have been very great, besides innumerable mansabdárs or petty vassals of less than a thousand horse; of whom, besides, there were 'never less than two or three hundred at Court.' These lower officers received from 150 to 700 rupees a month, and kept but two to six horses; and beneath them in rank were the *Rausandárs*, who were paid daily, and often filled the posts of clerks and secretaries. The troopers who formed the following of the Amírs and mansabdárs were entitled to the pay of 25 rupees a month for each horse, but did not always get it from their masters. Two horses to a man formed the usual allowance, for a one-horse trooper was regarded as little better than a one-legged man.

The possessions and lands of an Amír, as well as of the inferior classes of mansabdárs, were held only at the pleasure of the Emperor. When the grantee died, his title and all his property passed legally to the Crown, and his widows and children had to begin life again for themselves. The Emperor, however, was generally willing to make some provision for them out of the father's savings and extortionate peculations, and a mansabdár often managed to secure a grant for his sons during his own lifetime. Careful Amírs, or their heirs, moreover, were expert in the art of concealing their riches, so as to defeat the law of imperial inheritance; and it is a question whether Aurangzíb did not repudiate in practice, as he certainly did in writing, the obnoxious principle that the goods of the grantee should lapse to the Emperor to the exclusion of his natural heirs. The object, however, of keeping the control of the paid army, which these mansabdárs maintained, in the royal hands, was effectually secured by the temporary character of the rank.

The cavalry arm supplied by the Amírs and lesser mansabdárs and their retainers formed the chief part of the Mughal standing army, and, including the troops of the Rájput Rájas, who were also in receipt of an imperial subsidy, amounted in effective strength to more than 200,000 in Bernier's time (1659–66), of whom perhaps 40,000 were about the Emperor's person.

The regular infantry was of small account; the musketeers could only fire decently 'when squatting on the ground, and resting their muskets on a kind of wooden fork which hangs to them,' and were terribly afraid of burning their beards, or bursting their guns. There were about 15,000 of this arm about the Court, besides a larger number in the provinces; but the hordes of camp-followers, sutlers, grooms, traders, and servants, who always hung about the army, and were often absurdly reckoned as part of its effective strength, gave the impression of an infantry force of two or three hundred thousand men. All these people had directly or indirectly to be paid, and considering that there were few soldiers in the Mughal army who were not encumbered with wives, children, and slaves, it may be imagined that the army budget absorbed a very considerable part of the imperial revenue. There was also a small artillery arm, consisting partly of heavy guns, and partly of lighter pieces mounted on camels.

Whilst the Emperor kept the control of the army and nobles in his own hands by this system of grants of land or money in return for military service, the civil administration was governed on the same principle. Indeed, the civil and military characters were blended in the provincial administration. The *mansab* and *jágír* system pervaded the whole empire. The governors of provinces were mansabdárs, and received grants of land in lieu of salary for the maintenance of their state and their troops, and were required to pay about a fifth of the revenue to the Emperor[1]. All the land in the realm was thus parcelled out among a number of timariots, who were practically absolute in their own districts, and extorted the uttermost farthing from the wretched peasantry who tilled their lands. The only exceptions were the royal demesnes, and these were farmed out to contractors who had all the vices without the distinctions of the mansabdárs. As it was always the policy of the Mughals to frequently shift the vassal-lords from one estate to another, in order to prevent their acquiring a permanent local influence and prestige, the same disastrous results ensued as in the precarious appointments of Turkey. Each governor or feudatory sought to exact all he could possibly get out of his province or jágír, in order to have capital in hand when he should be transplanted or deprived of his estate. Their authority in the outlying districts was to all intents and purposes supreme, for no appeal from their tyranny and oppression existed except to the Emperor himself, and they took good care that their proceedings should not be reported at Court. The local kázís or judges were the tools of the governor, and the imperial inspectors doubtless had their price for silence. Near Delhi or Agra or any of the larger towns such oppression and corruption could scarcely be concealed, and Aurangzíb's well-known love of justice would have instantly inflicted condign punishment: but in

[1] See below, p. 124.

the remoter parts of the Empire the cruelty and rapacity of the landholders went on almost unchecked. The peasantry and working classes, and even the better sort of merchants, used every precaution to hide such small prosperity as they might enjoy; they dressed and lived meanly, and suppressed all inclinations to raise themselves socially in the scale of civilization. Very often they were driven to seek refuge in neighbouring lands, or took service under a native Rája who had a little more mercy to people of his own faith than could be expected from a Muhammadan adventurer.

Such was the administrative system of the Mughal Empire in the time of Aurangzíb. In principle it was the same as in the days of Akbar; the difference lay only in the choice of an inferior, ill-educated class of Muslim officials, to the general exclusion of the more capable Hindús, and in the inadequate measures taken for local inspection and supervision. Aurangzíb himself strove to be a righteous ruler, but he was either afraid of arousing the discontent of his vassals by stringent supervision, or he was unable to secure the probity of a faithful body of inspectors. In either case the fact remains that while the central government was rigidly just and righteous, in the Muhammadan acceptation of law, the provincial administration was generally venal and oppressive. Whether we look at the military or the civil aspect of the system, it is clear that the Mughal domination in India was even more in the nature of an army of occupation than the 'camp' to which the Ottoman Empire has been compared. As Bernier says, 'The Great Mogul is a foreigner in Hindústán: he finds himself in a hostile country, or nearly so; a country containing hundreds of Gentiles to one Mughal, or even to one Muhammadan.' Hence his large armies; his network of feudatory governors and landholders dependent upon his countenance alone for their dignity and support; hence, too, an administrative policy which sacrificed the welfare of the people to the supremacy of an armed minority. Had the people been other than Hindús, accustomed to oppression, the system would have broken down. As it was, it preserved internal peace, and secured the authority of the throne during a long and critical reign. We read of few disturbances or insurrections in all these fifty years. Such wars as were waged were either campaigns of aggression outside the normal limits of the Empire, or were deliberately provoked by the Emperor's intolerance.

The external wars are of little historical significance. Mír Jumla's disastrous campaign in Assam was typical of many other attempts to subdue the north-east frontagers of India. The rains and the guerilla tactics of the enemy drove the Mughal army to despair, and its gallant leader died on his return in the spring of 1663. 'You mourn,' said Aurangzíb to Mír Jumla's son, 'you mourn a loving father, and I the most powerful and the most dangerous of my friends.' The war in Arakán had more lasting effects. That kingdom had long been a standing menace to Bengal, and a cause of loss and dread to the traders at the mouths of the Ganges. Every kind of criminal from Goa or Ceylon, Cochin or Malacca, mostly Portuguese or half-castes, flocked to Chittagong, where the King of Arakán, delighted to welcome any sort of allies against his formidable neighbour the Mughal, permitted them to settle. They soon developed a busy trade in piracy; 'scoured the neighbouring seas in light galleys, called galleasses, entered the numerous arms and branches of the Ganges, ravaged the islands of Lower Bengal, and, often penetrating forty or fifty leagues up the country, surprised and carried away the entire population of villages. The marauders made slaves of their unhappy captives, and burnt whatever could not be removed[1].' The Portuguese settled at the Húglí had abetted these rascals by purchasing whole cargoes of cheap slaves, and had been punished for these and other misdeeds in an exemplary manner by Sháh-Jahán, who took their town and carried the whole Portuguese population captive to Agra (1630). But though the Portuguese power no longer availed them, the pirates went on with their rapine, and carried on operations with even greater vigour from the island of Sandíp, off Chittagong, where 'the notorious Fra Joan, an Augustinian monk, reigned as a petty sovereign during many years, having contrived, God knows how, to rid himself of the governor of the island.' It was these freebooters who had sailed up to Dhakká, and enabled

[1] Bernier, pp. 174–182.

Prince Shujá' to escape with them to Arakán, robbing him secretly on the way.

When Sháyista Khán came as Governor to Bengal, in succession to Mír Jumla, he judged it high time to put a stop to these exploits, besides punishing the King of Arakán for his treachery to Shujá', who, though a rival, was Aurangzíb's brother, and as such not to be treated with disrespect. Strange to relate, the pirates submitted at once to the summons of the Bengal governor (1666), backed as it was by the support of the Dutch, who were pleased to help in anything that might still further diminish the failing power of Portugal. The bulk of the freebooters were settled under rigorous supervision at a place a few miles below Dhakká, hence called Firingi-bázár, 'the mart of the Franks,' where some of their descendants still live. Sháyista then sent an expedition against Arakán and annexed it, changing the name of Chittagong into Islámábád, 'the city of Islám.' He little knew that in suppressing piracy in the Gulf of Bengal he was materially assisting the rise of that future power, whose coming triumphs could scarcely have been foretold from the humble beginnings of the little factory established by the English at the Húglí in 1640. Just twenty years after the suppression of the Portuguese, Job Charnock defeated the local forces of the faujdár, and in 1690 received from Aurangzíb, whose revenue was palpably suffering from the loss of trade and customs involved in such hostilities, a grant of land at Sutánatí, which he immediately cleared of jungle and fortified. Such was the modest foundation of Calcutta. The growth of the East India Company's power, however, belongs to the period of the decline of the Mughal Empire: whilst Aurangzíb lived, the disputes with the English traders were insignificant.

CHAPTER VII

The Revenue

It may well be asked what resources the Emperor possessed to defray the cost of his splendid Court, to provide the immense sums required for the salaries of the nobles and mansabdárs, and to maintain the vast standing army and multitudinous civil staff of the Empire. The revenue of the Mughal Emperors has recently been the subject of controversy, and I may be pardoned if I am therefore obliged to enter into somewhat minute details. A good many returns of the actual sums annually paid by each province to the imperial exchequer have been preserved, both by Native and European contemporaries, and of the consistency and rough accuracy of these returns there can be no doubt whatever. The controversy which has been raised does not impugn their credibility, but merely relates to two points: first, the conversion of the Indian revenue into English money of the time; and secondly, the question whether these returns include the gross revenue from all sources, or merely the income from the land-tax.

The former difficulty is easily disposed of. The average value of the rupee at the period, covered by the returns, from 1594 to 1707 was 2s. 3*d.* in English money of the time. The value of the rupee varied a little with the condition of the coin. If much worn it fell to perhaps 2s.; if quite new and of full weight it may have been worth as much as 2s. 6*d.*; but that 2s. 3*d.* was the ordinary rate of exchange is abundantly clear from numerous records [1]. Mr. H. G. Keene, the able historian of Hindústán, has fallen into the error of estimating the rupee as low as 1s. 3*d.*, from a mistaken valuation of the French *livre*, which he would make equivalent to 10*d.* Apart from the fact that we have Bailly's authority for estimating the *livre* of the period at 1s. 6*d.*, it is inconceivable that English travellers should have exchanged their money at the rate of 2s. 3*d.* for the rupee, whilst French travellers of the same period should have obtained the rupee for 1s. 3*d.* We may be perfectly certain

[1] The following are some of the chief estimates: 1615, Sir Thomas Roe, 2s. 2*d.*; Terry, 2s. to 2s. 9*d.*; 1638, Mandelslo, ½ *écu*; 1640–67, Tavernier, ½ *écu* or 1½ *livre* or 30 *sols*, which the English translator of 1684 renders by 2s. 3*d.*; 1659–66, Bernier, 30 *sols*; 1666, Thevenot, 30 *sols*; 1673, Fryer, 2s. 3*d.*; 1689, Ovington, 2s. 3*d.*; 1697, Manucci, 30 *sols*. The *écu* was 3 *livres*, and the *livre* contained 20 *sols*. The *livre tournois* of 1643-61 (i. e. the *livre* of account as known to Bernier, Tavernier, and Thevenot) was worth 1·95 *francs*, and that of 1684–1715 (i. e. that of Manucci) a trifle less (1·80), according to Bailly's *Hist. financière de la France*, vol. ii. p. 298. The *livre* was thus equal to about 1s. 6*d.* This agrees with Sir Isaac Newton's estimate of the *écu* at 4s. 6*d.* in 1717. See also J. A. Blanchet, *Nouveau Manuel de Numismatique* (1890), vol. i. p. 26. The rupee, estimated at ½ *écu* or 1½ *livre* or 30 *sols* by Mandelslo, Tavernier, Bernier, Thevenot, and Manucci, was therefore equal to 2s. 3*d.* English.

that when Dr. Fryer and the Rev. John Ovington changed their money in 1673 and 1689, they got as good value for it as Bernier in 1666, or Manucci in 1697. So great a discrepancy as is involved in Mr. Keene's estimate of the French *livre* is clearly inadmissable.

The fiscal unit of the Native returns is the *dám*, and forty *dáms* went to the rupee: of this there is no dispute. The European returns are given in rupees, which may be taken, as I have said, on the average at 2s. 3*d*., or in *livres* of about the value of 1s. 6*d*. Reducing *dáms* to rupees, and rupees and *livres* to pounds, in accordance with these values, we obtain the following returns of the annual revenue for different years[1], expressed in round figures:—

		£	
Akbar	1594	18,640,000	(Abu-l-Fazl)
„	1605	19,630,000	(De Laët)
Jahángír	1627	19,680,000	(Bádsháh-náma)
Sháh-Jahán	1628	18,750,000	(Muh. Sharíf)
„	1648	24,750,000	(Bádsháh-náma)
„	1655	30,080,000	(Official returns)
Aurangzíb	1660 *circ.*	25,410,000	(Bernier)
„	1666	26,700,000	(Thevenot)
„	1667 *circ.*	30,850,000	(Bakhtáwar)
„	later	40,100,000	(Official returns)
„	1697	43,550,000	(Manucci)
„	1707	33,950,000	(Ramusio)

The preceding figures show a reasonable and

[1] The authorities from which the returns are derived will be found fully described in the late Mr. Edward Thomas's penetrating essay *The Revenue Resources of the Mughal Empire in India* (1871), with the exception of those for 1628, and *circa* 1667, which I have taken from the *Majális as-Salátín* of Muhammad Sharíf Hanafí, and from Bakhtáwar Khán, respectively.

consistent progress in the prosperity of the Empire. The increase in 1655 is explained by the addition of the tribute from the Deccan kingdoms. The decrease in revenue about 1660 and in 1707 is satisfactorily explained by the civil war and ensuing famine which accompanied Aurangzíb's accession in 1658, and the protracted campaigns and losses in the Deccan which preceded his death in 1707. The figures here given[1] are in excess of those stated by the late distinguished numismatist, Mr. Edward Thomas, in proportion as the rupee is here valued at *2s. 3d.*, instead of at his admittedly conventional estimate of *2s.*

We may take it, therefore, that the revenue returns of the Mughal Emperors show a steady increase from about £19,000,000 towards the end of Akbar's reign, to over £40,000,000 when Aurangzíb was at the height of his power. The *second* disputed question here arises: Do these returns include every regular source of income, or do they merely relate to the revenue from land? The answer must be unhesitating: they represent only the land revenue, including, however, the tribute which took the place of the land-tax in those half-subdued States where the imperial collector did not penetrate. Bernier and Manucci distinctly state that the returns they quote relate only to the revenue from land, and, though the Native historians do not qualify their returns by any such

[1] I have neglected certain variations in the returns caused by the subtraction of the tax-gatherer's percentage, which amounted to 4 per cent. in Aurangzíb's time, but was higher under Akbar.

statement, it is obvious that, writing for Natives only, they would pre-suppose that the system of the imperial accounts was familiar to their readers. It is evident that, since Bernier's £25,410,000 about 1660 refers only to the land-revenue, the £24,750,000 mentioned in the Bádsháh-náma of 'Abd-al-Hamíd Láhorí in 1648 must be limited to the same class of revenue; and by the same reasoning the £40,000,000 of the official records (*dastur-i-'amal*) of about the middle of Aurangzíb's reign cannot include a wider basis of revenue than Manucci's £43,550,000 of 1697. The whole series of returns is consistent, and the fact that two of them are distinctly restricted to the land-tax limits the whole series to the same source of revenue.

The Mughal Emperors, therefore, drew from land alone a revenue rising from about 19 millions in 1600 to 43 millions in 1700. The Emperor was titular lord of the soil, but in practice he restricted his interest to levying a tax of about one-third the gross produce. Akbar established an admirable agricultural department, and laid down rules for periodical valuations of the land, and for the allowance to be made for impoverishment, bad seasons, and the like. These rules prevailed in the reign of Aurangzíb, and though they may have been largely evaded by corrupt officials in remote districts, there is no doubt that the system was equitable in theory, and was strictly enforced wherever the Emperor's influence and inspection reached. In the present day the revenue from the land is about

24 millions; but the British government is contented with less than $\frac{1}{10}$th of the gross produce, instead of $\frac{1}{3}$rd. Were the Mughal third exacted, the present land tax of British India (which is of course a much larger area than Mughal India) would probably amount to 80 millions.

Some idea may be formed of the surplus of the land revenue over the expenses of administration, from a statement in the *Mir-át-i 'A'lam* ascribed to Bakhtáwar Khán or Muhammad Baká. This history fixes the revenue at 9,24,17,16,082 *dáms* (about £30,850,000), and adds 'out of which the Khálisa, or sum paid to the Royal Treasury, is 1,72,79,81,251 *dáms*, and the assignments of the *jágírdárs* [or grantees of the lands], or the balance, is 7,51,77,34,731 *dáms*.' There is a slight error in the arithmetic, but the important deduction may be drawn that, after paying the cost of administration, including the high salaries of the mansabdárs, to whom the estates were assigned as jágírs, about a sixth to a fifth of the total land revenue accrued as surplus to the imperial exchequer.

To arrive at any definite estimate of the *gross* revenue is impossible, owing to the fluctuating character of the taxation apart from the rent drawn from land. The Mughal Emperors were constantly remitting taxes, but it is not clear how far these remissions were temporary, or whether their place was taken by other imposts. A list of thirty-eight taxes remitted or reduced by Akbar is given in the *Áín-i Akbarí*, some of which were certainly restored or increased by the time of Aurangzíb's accession. That Emperor himself began his reign by remitting nearly eighty taxes, to relieve the poverty produced by the civil war and the famine that followed it. These taxes are vaguely stated by Kháfí Khán to have 'brought in crores of rupees to the public treasury[1].' But it is added that the local officials paid little heed to the imperial edict of remission. Later in the reign, all import duties on the goods of Muhammadan traders were abolished; but this was modified in so far that the 5 p. c. duty on Hindú goods was reduced to 2½ p. c. on those of Muhammadans. It is evident that the numerous tolls, taxes, and cesses outside the land-tax were variable sources of revenue, and no returns of their totals seem to have been preserved. Again, one would expect a considerable rise in the revenue after the re-imposition of the *jizya* or poll-tax in or about 1675; for it is recorded that the city of Burhánpúr alone paid 26,000 rupees on account of this tax, and the total for all Hindústán must have been enormous, if the tax was ever strictly enforced, which is doubtful. Of the sum derived from this and all other taxes, except the land-tax, the native historians give no definite account. Nor are we able to form any estimate of the amount received from the Emperor's title to the effects of the mansabdárs from confiscations, or from that perennial source of wealth, the constant and

[1] *Muntakhab-al-lubáb*, in Elliot and Dowson, vol. vii. p. 247.

costly presents of money and jewels which it was the custom of every noble, every official, every suitor, and every traveller, to offer to the Great Mogul. Tavernier's present to Aurangzíb on one single occasion amounted in value to 12,119 *livres*, or over £900, and this was a trifle compared with the vast sums presented by the nobles to his Majesty on his birthday and other occasions.

But if detailed returns of these numerous sources of income are wanting, we have three separate statements by Europeans which may guide us to a rough estimate of the gross revenue. Their consistency adds to their probability; but they are only vague guesses at the best. The first is the statement by William Hawkins, who lived on intimate terms with Jahángír from 1609 to 1611, that the Emperor's revenue was fifty crores of rupees (£56,000,000). It is true he damages his evidence by saying that this was the King's 'yearly income of his crown land,' which is manifestly absurd in the face of other returns already quoted: but if the 50,00,00,000 rupees be taken to mean the gross revenue from all sources, or more than double the revenue from land, it is not perhaps much exaggerated. The second statement is that of Catrou or his authority Manucci (the two are unfortunately inseparable), who, referring to 1697, says that the recorded revenue of 43½ millions is derived solely from the fruits of the earth, and that the 'casuel' or extraordinary and fluctuating revenue, '*égale, à peu près, ou surpasse même* les immenses richesses qui l'Empereur perçoit des seuls fonds de terre de son Domaine[1].' This 'casuel' consisted of the *jizya*, or poll-tax on Hindús, the transport customs and port dues, the tax on the 'blanchissage de cette multitude infinie de toiles qu'on travaille aux Indes,' the royalty on diamond mines, the royal right of inheritance of all official estates, and the tribute of various Rájas. Catrou is not able to give details of these receipts, save in one instance. He mentions that the port dues of Súrat amounted to thirty lacs, and the tax on the mint-profits of the same city to eleven lacs of rupees. In other words Súrat contributed something like half-a-million sterling in addition to the land tax. At this rate it is not difficult to believe that the 'casuel' revenue amounted to as large an income as that derived from the land. The third statement is that of Dr. Gemelli Careri, who visited Aurangzíb in the Deccan in 1695, and 'was told' that the Emperor's revenue 'from only his hereditary countries' was eighty crores of rupees (or ninety millions of pounds). Now we have already seen that in 1697 the land revenue amounted to 43½ millions. Careri's estimate of the gross revenue is therefore equivalent to rather more than double the land tax, which accords very accurately with Catrou's statement that the 'casuel' was as much as, or more than, the land revenue, and with Hawkins' rough record of Jahángír's income of fifty crores or more than double the land tax of his

[1] Catrou, *Histoire générale de l'Empire du Mogol*, (1715), p. 267.

time. Careri's qualification that this revenue of eighty crores was derived only from Aurangzíb's 'hereditary countries' does not in any way confuse the result, for it is unlikely that he drew much from the Deccan during the stormy period of conquest and devastation, and extremely improbable that he drew even as much as the ten crores which formed the tribute from Bíjápúr and Golkonda in Catrou's total of 43½ millions of revenue. From the three statements[1] of Hawkins, Catrou, and Careri, we may conclude that the gross revenue from all sources was equal to at least double the land revenue of the Great Mogul, and to obtain the total income we must double the sums given in the returns quoted above. In other words the gross revenue of the Mughal Empire may be taken at fully £36,000,000 in 1594, and gradually rose to £90,000,000 in 1695.

[1] I have not mentioned Thomas's theory that the gross income of Akbar in 1593 was (at 2s. 3d. the rupee) £36,000,000, because it is based on the assumption that the 640,00,00,000 *murádí tankas* of Nizám-ad-dín Ahmad's return for that year (which I have purposely omitted in the list given above) were equivalent to *double dáms.* The terms *dám* and *tanka* are interchangeable, as is proved by the inscriptions on the coins themselves, and though there were undoubtedly double dams, as well as double tankas, there is really no valid ground for assuming in this single instance a different fiscal unit from that employed in all the other returns. Thomas's doubling of the 640 crores in 1593 is, moreover, rendered still more improbable by the fact that 662 crores form the total for 1594—a perfectly possible increase. I therefore take Nizám-ad-dín's return to represent £18,000,000. Whilst disbelieving in the *murádí tanka* theory, however, as a ground for the higher estimate, I do not doubt that the *gross* revenue of Akbar in 1593 may have been quite thirty-six millions.

'Doubtless,' remarks Catrou, 'such prodigious wealth is amazing; but it must be remembered that all these riches only enter the Mughal treasury to go out again, at least in part, every year, and flow again over the land. Half the empire subsists on the bounty of the Emperor or at least is in his keep. Besides the multitude of officers and soldiers who live by their pay, all the rural peasantry, who toil only for the sovereign, are supported at his cost, and almost all the artisans of the towns, who are made to work for the Mughal, are paid out of the royal exchequer.'

When it is remembered that one Mughal Amír, and that an honest one, is recorded to have saved 'nearly 5000 crowns a month,' or more than £13,000 a year, out of his allowance as 'Amír of 5000,' it will be readily understood how enormous were the outgoings of the treasury for the support of the life-peers alone. In spite of his immense revenue, the expenditure of a Mughal Emperor was so prodigious that he was able to save little. Notwithstanding all his hoardings, and his long reign of peace, Sháh-Jahán 'never amassed six crores of rupees,' apart from jewels and ornaments, whilst Aurangzíb left only thirteen lacs, or less than £150,000 in the treasury when he died, and was frequently hard pressed to find the money for the pay of his army.

CHAPTER VIII

The Hindús

The expeditions into Assam and Arakán did not disturb the general peace of Hindústán. A profound tranquillity, broken by no rebellion of any political importance, reigned throughout northern India for the first twenty years of Aurangzíb's rule. The Deccan troubles, which will be described later, awoke no corresponding excitement in the north. So quiet, indeed, was the country, so absolute the security of the crown, that Aurangzíb was able with an easy mind to allow himself a rest and change of scene, after the dangerous illness which prostrated him in 1664. Leaving his father still a captive at Agra, but fearing no revolution in his behalf, the Emperor set out in December, 1664, upon the journey to Kashmír, of which Bernier has preserved a vivid diary. The holiday was to last eighteen months, at least six of which were consumed in coming and going. The Mughal travelled in a leisurely manner, as befitted his state, and often stopped for a few days' hunting, or deviated from the direct route to search for water. It would have been impossible to hurry with such an unwieldy following as always accompanied the Emperor on his journeys. His regular body-guard of 35,000 horsemen of course went with him, besides over 10,000 infantry, and the heavy and light artillery, consisting of 100 or 120 brass pieces, some of which were dragged over the rugged places of the road with considerable difficulty. A large body of Amírs and Rájas and lesser vassals was always in close attendance on the royal person, mounted on horseback, to their infinite disgust, instead of their usual comfortable palankins. The Emperor himself travelled either in a throne borne on men's shoulders, or mounted on his horse or elephant:—

> 'Imperial Delhi op'ning wide her Gates,
> Pours out her thronging Legions, bright in Arms,
> And all the Pomp of War. Before them sound
> Clarions and Trumpets, breathing Martial Airs
> And bold Defiance. High upon his Throne,
> Borne on the Back of his proud Elephant,
> Sits the great Chief of Tamur's glorious Race:
> Sublime he sits, amid the radiant Blaze
> Of Gems and Gold. *Omrahs* about him crowd,
> And rein th' *Arabian* steed, and watch his Nod:
> And potent *Rajahs*, who themselves preside
> O'er Realms of wide Extent; but here submiss
> Their Homage pay, alternate Kings and Slaves.
> Next these with prying Eunuchs girt around,
> The fair Sultanas of his Court; a Troop
> Of chosen Beauties, but with Care concealed
> From each intrusive Eye; one Look is Death[1].'

The Seraglio formed a striking feature in the procession, with the gilded and silken palankins and

[1] Somervile, *The Chace*, Bk. ii. ('Constable's Oriental Miscellany,' vol. iii. p. 208).

travelling couches of the princesses, the gorgeous litters hung between two camels or elephants, or the high howdahs loaded with eight women, and covered with rich silks and embroidery.

'I cannot avoid dwelling on this pompous procession of the Seraglio,' wrote Bernier. 'Stretch imagination to its utmost limits, and you can imagine no exhibition more grand and imposing than when Raushan-Árá Begam, mounted on a stupendous Pegu elephant, and seated in a *meghdambhár* blazing with gold and azure, is followed by five or six elephants with *meghdambhárs* nearly as resplendent as her own, and filled with ladies attached to her household, [and succeeded by the most distinguished ladies of the Court] until fifteen or sixteen females of quality pass with a grandeur of appearance, equipage and retinue, more or less proportionate to their rank, pay, and office. There is something very impressive of state and royalty in the march of these sixty or more elephants; in their solemn and as it were measured steps, in the splendour of the *meghdambhárs*, and the brilliant and innumerable followers in attendance: and if I had not regarded this display of magnificence with a sort of philosophical indifference, I should have been apt to be carried away by such flights of imagination as inspire most of the Indian poets, when they represent the elephants as conveying so many goddesses concealed from the vulgar gaze[1].'

Bernier was fortunate in seeing so much of the procession, for it was as much as a man's life was worth to be found too near the Seraglio, and once the French doctor had to fight his way through the eunuchs, sword in hand, to escape a merciless beating.

[1] Bernier, pp. 372-3.

Besides these important members of his family and suite, the Emperor's march was followed by an innumerable multitude of servants and tradespeople. Indeed the whole of Delhi turned out to follow its customers, since there was no alternative but to join the procession of its sole employers or to stay at home and starve in a deserted city. The same tradesmen who kept shop in town, were obliged to keep shop in the field, while

> Delhi mourns
> Her empty and depopulated Streets.

The total number of persons in the camp was estimated at between three and four hundred thousand. They had to carry all necessaries with them, except forage; for to pillage the country they passed through, would have been to rob the Emperor, who was, at least in theory, its sole owner; and but for the extreme simplicity of the Indian soldiers' diet and their avoidance of animal food, the camp must have exhibited a scene of appalling starvation. The usual Eastern plan of double camps was observed, one to sleep in, the other, called *Paish-khána*, to go on in front to be pitched ready for the following night. In each was pitched a travelling Audience and Presence Chamber, where the Emperor held his daily levees and councils, under silk and velvet canopies, exactly as he did at Delhi or Agra. The royal tents were red, lined with hand-painted chintz from Masulipatan, beautifully embroidered and fringed with gold and silver and silk; and the tent poles were painted and gilt. Hard by the Emperor's were the Begams' tents. The whole was enclosed in a square fenced in with wooden screens; and outside the gate were the quarters of the guard, the music, and the principal officers of state, while the smaller folk ranged their tents at proper distances, the entire camp forming a circle of about five or six miles' circumference. Over all, shone the light of the Akásdiah, or Lamp of Heaven, an imperial beacon, consisting of a lantern hanging at the top of a mast forty yards high, to guide wanderers to their tents by night, while watch-fires blazed round the camp and the sentinel paced his silent round.

On his return from his long repose in Kashmír, where he seems to have spent the greater part of 1665, Aurangzíb found his empire as tranquil as he had left it, and a source of danger was removed early in 1666 by the death of his father Sháh-Jahán in his splendid prison at Agra. The news of Sháyista Khán's successes in Arakán reached him in the same year, and the most troublesome of his antagonists in the Deccan, the Maráthá Sivají, made his submission and actually ventured to present himself at Court. Soon afterwards, in 1668, the greatest of the friendly but formidable Rájput Rájas died: Jai Singh, who had been a loyal and energetic servant of the Emperor ever since his accession, and had led many a campaign in the Deccan at the head of his valiant tribesmen. The other famous Rájput general, Jaswant Singh, was far away in his government at Kábul, and was also approaching his end. At last the Emperor was free to carry out the repressive policy towards the Hindús which must be the aim of every good Muslim. So far there had been no persecution, no religious disabilities: but there can be no doubt that Aurangzíb was only nursing his zeal for the Faith, until it should be safe to display it against the unbelievers.

It seems to have been in 1669 that the storm began to gather[1]. In April of that year Aurangzíb was informed that the Bráhmans of Benáres and other Hindú centres were in the habit of teaching their 'wicked sciences,' not only to their own people but to Muslims. This was more than the orthodox Emperor could tolerate; but the severity of his measures shows that he had been only waiting for a pretext to come down like a thunderbolt upon the unfortunate 'heathen.' 'The Director of the Faith,' we are told, 'issued orders to all the governors of provinces to destroy with a willing hand the schools and temples of the infidels: and they were strictly enjoined to put an entire stop to the teaching and practising of idolatrous forms of worship.' It is not for a moment to be supposed that these orders were literally carried out. Even the English Government would not dare to risk such an experiment in India. All that was done was to make a few signal examples, and thus to warn the Bráhmans from attempting to make proselytes among the True

[1] The first notice of any religious persecution occurs in the *Maásir-i Álamgíri* of Musta'idd Khán, under the date 17 Zú-l-ka'da 1079 (18 April, 1669); but the dates become very hazy after Aurangzíb's prohibition of official chronicles in the eleventh year of his reign.

Believers. With this object the temple of Vishnu at Benáres was destroyed and a splendid shrine at Mathura was razed to the ground, to make room for a magnificent mosque. The idols found in the temples were brought to Agra and buried under the steps of the mosque, so that good Muslims might have the satisfaction of treading them under foot.

Three years later the fanaticism of the Hindús found vent in an insurrection of four or five thousand devotees, who called themselves Satnámís, in Mewát, which gave the imperial officers no little trouble to subdue. The quarrel arose from a blow given by one of the Government inspectors, but the hostility of the sect must have been already at fever-heat to fire up at so slight a provocation. The Satnámís assembled in their thousands, wreaked their vengeance on the officials, occupied Nárnól, and began to levy the taxes and administer the district themselves. The ordinary provincial forces were repeatedly worsted; even several expeditions despatched from Delhi only met the rioters to be discomfited and put to flight. 'It was said that swords, arrows, and musket balls had no effect on these men, and that every arrow and ball which they discharged brought down two or three men. Thus they were credited with magic and witchcraft, and were said to have magic wooden horses like live ones, on which their women rode as an advanced guard [1].' The neighbouring Rájputs and other Hindús began to become infected with the spirit of rebellion,

[1] Kháfí Khán, *l. c.* vol. vii. p. 295.

and every day saw fresh additions to the strength of the rioters.

Aurangzíb saw that his troops were demoralized by fear of the enemy's supposed magic, and he resolved to counteract witchcraft by holy charms. He wrote some pious texts, and had them sewn to his banners. To him, the device probably meant no more than the expression of his zeal: 'In the name of the Lord will I destroy them.' But to his soldiers the blessed words from the Korán were sure amulets against the sorcery of the enemy. Led by Persian nobles, always keen to do battle with Hindús, the imperial troops fell upon the badly armed rebels like avenging zealots, and soon the conflict became a massacre. The Satnámís fought with the courage of despair and the exaltation of martyrs, but the end was not doubtful: thousands were slain; and the insurrection was suppressed.

It is very difficult to trace the cause and effect of Aurangzíb's successive steps in his reactionary policy towards the Hindús. In the eleventh year of his reign he suddenly put a stop to the system of official chronicles, which had been minutely recorded by historiographers royal since the time of Akbar. Now, it was strictly forbidden to write any chronicles at all, and those that have come down to us were recorded in secret, or merely treasured in the memory, and have all the confusion and fragmentary character of haphazard reminiscences. There are probably several links missing in the chain of events which connected the first destruction of Hindú temples in 1669 with the imposition of the hated *jizya* or poll-tax on unbelievers, a few years later[1]. The revolt of the Satnámís is one of the few links that have been preserved by the secret chroniclers, who were naturally disinclined to soil their pens with the doings of 'unclean infidels.' Another event is the rash interference of the Emperor in the matter of Jaswant Singh's children.

The death of a powerful Rája would naturally lead to a fresh encroachment against the Hindús, and the desire of Aurangzíb to meddle in the family affairs of the Rájputs is a sign that he felt himself strong enough to impose a strict Muhammadan rule all over India. He was not deterred by the hostile demonstrations which the re-imposition of the hated poll-tax aroused at Delhi. In vain the people wailed and cursed around the palace. Aurangzíb had by this time abandoned the salutary custom of appearing at stated hours before his subjects at the levee window: the adulation of the multitude savoured of idolatry to his puritanical mind. But seclude himself as he might—and thereby lose the sensitive touch of the populace which had been his father's strength—he could not shut his eyes to the uproar which the new enactment excited. When he

[1] Dr. Fryer, writing in 1675, mentions the *new tax* on Hindús, which, he says, amounted to as much as a gold mohur, or 31*s.* 6*d.* for a Bráhman. Manucci states that the tax ranged from 3½ rupees levied on the poor to 13½ on merchants, i.e. from about 8*s.* to 30*s.* 4*d.*

went to the mosque, crowds of expostulating and even riotous Hindús blocked his way; and though his elephants forced their way over their bodies, he could not subdue their invincible repugnance to the new instrument of bigotry. His dealings with the Rájput princes kindled these sparks of discontent into a flame. He endeavoured to get Jaswant Singh's two sons sent to Delhi to be educated, and doubtless made Muslims. under his own supervision. Of course the Rájputs would not hear of this: their loyalty and their pride alike forbade such ignominy to their hereditary chiefs. And when they learned that the bigoted Emperor had revived the ancient law of Muhammad which imposed a tax upon every soul who did not conform to Islám —a tax which Akbar had disdained, and Sháh-Jahán had not dared to think of—their indignation knew no bounds. They repudiated the religious tax, and they contrived to spirit away the infant princes of Márwár out of the Emperor's reach.

It was the first serious rebellion during the reign. and its provoker little realized the effects which his fanatical policy would produce. He marched at once upon Rájputána, where he found two out of the three leading States, Údaipúr (Mewár) and Jodhpúr (Márwár) united against him, and only Rája Rám Singh of Jaipúr (Amber) still loyal to the empire. The Rájputs kept 25,000 horse, mostly Ráhtors of Jodhpúr, in the field, and although frequently driven into their mountains were never really subdued. At one time they seemed to be at the point of a decisive victory, and the Emperor's cause appeared lost. Directing operations from Ajmír, he had placed his main body under his fourth son Akbar, at the same time calling up his elder sons Mu'azzam and A'zam with their contingents from their commands in the Deccan and Bengal. The three princes were busy ravaging the Rájput country, and Aurangzíb was left at Ajmír with hardly a thousand men, when tidings came that Prince Akbar had been seduced by the diplomacy of the Rájput leaders, had gone over with the main army to the enemy, and proclaimed himself Emperor of India; nay, more, he was now marching upon his father at the head of 70,000 men. Aurangzíb must have thought of the fate of Sháh-Jahán, and feared that it was now his turn to make room for an ambitious son: but his presence of mind did not desert him even at this crisis. Summoning Prince Mu'azzam to come to his aid with such troops as he could gather, the Emperor essayed a counter-move in the game of diplomacy. He wrote a letter congratulating the rebel Prince upon his success in deceiving the Rájputs and luring them on to their destruction, and contrived that this compromising epistle should be intercepted by one of the rebellious Rájas[1]. The effect of his plot exceeded all expectations. The Mughal deserters flocked back to the imperial standard, led

[1] Kháfí Khán questions the accuracy of this story. It is clear, however, that by some means Aurangzíb contrived to win back the deserters, and the letter is as probable a ruse as any other.

by their repentant general Tuhawwar Khán, who was at once decapitated; the Rájput army melted away; and Prince Akbar, with a following of 500 men, fled to the Deccan (June, 1681), and became the guest of the Maráthá chief at Ráhirí, whence he eventually sailed for Persia, and never again set foot in the realm of his fathers.

The Rájput snake was scotched, but far from killed. The insults which had been offered to their chiefs and their religion, the ruthless and unnecessary severity of Aurangzíb's campaigns in their country, left a sore which never healed. A race which had been the right arm of the Mughal empire at the beginning of the reign was now hopelessly alienated, and never again served the throne without distrust. The war went on. The Mughals ravaged the rich lands of Údaipúr, and the Rájputs retaliated by throwing down mosques and insulting the Muslims. The cities were indeed in the hands of Aurangzíb, but the mountain defiles were thronged with implacable foes, who lost no opportunity of dealing a blow at the invaders. The Rána of Údaipúr, who was the chief sufferer on the Rájput side, succeeded at last in making an honourable peace with Aurangzíb, who was tired of the struggle and anxious to give his whole mind to his affairs in the Deccan. The hated *jizya* was not even named in the treaty; a small cession of territory was made by the Rána as an indemnity for siding with Prince Akbar; and Jaswant Singh's son, the young Rája of Jodhpúr, was acknowledged heir to his father's principality. But while the treaty enabled Aurangzíb to beat a fairly creditable retreat, it did not appease the indignant Rájputs of the west; even the Rána of Údaipúr soon rode his elephants through the treaty; and all Rájputána, save Jaipúr and the eastern parts, was perpetually in a state of revolt until the end of the reign. *Tantum relligio potuit!* But for his tax upon heresy, and his interference with their inborn sense of dignity and honour, Aurangzíb might have still kept the Rájputs by his side as priceless allies in the long struggle in which he was now to engage in the Deccan. As it was he alienated them for ever. No Rájput Rája would again marshall his willing mountaineers to support a Mughal throne, as had been seen in the days of Jai Singh. So long as the great Puritan sat on the throne of Akbar, not a Rájput would stir a finger to save him. Aurangzíb had to fight his southern foes with the loss of his right arm.

CHAPTER IX

THE DECCAN

'DELHI is distant,' says an old Deccan proverb, and many an Indian king has realized its force, when grappling with the ineradicable contumacy of his southern province. The Deccan (Dakhin, Dak-han, 'the South') was never intended by nature to have any connexion with Hindústán. The Vindhya and Satpúra mountains and the Narbadá river form a triple line of natural barricades, which divide the high table-land of Central India from the plains of the Ganges and its tributaries, and should have warned the sovereigns of Delhi that it was wiser to keep to their own country. But the Deccan lands were fertile; their wealth in gold and diamonds was fabulous; and every great ruler of the northern plains has turned his eyes to the mountain barriers and longed to enter the land of promise beyond. They entered, however, at their peril. To conquer the Deccan was another phrase for risking the loss of Hindústán; for he who invaded the southern people who dwelt between the Gháts was in danger of teaching them the road to the north.

The first Muhammadan sovereign who brought the whole of the Deccan under the sway of Delhi was Muhammad ibn Taghlak, in the fourteenth century. His sagacity and eccentricity were equally displayed in his choice of a new capital and in his singular mode of supplying it with a ready-made population. He wisely fixed upon Deogíri, on account of its central situation—for in those days, at least, before railways and telegraphs, he who would rule the Deccan must live there;—and he ruthlessly transported the whole population of Delhi backwards and forwards, between his old and his new capital, henceforth to be known as Daulatábád, or 'Empire-city.' His death put an end to the dominion of the north over the south, and a great Afghán dynasty, the Bahmaní kings, took possession of the Deccan. About the close of the fifteenth century their broad dominions were split up into five distinct kingdoms, of which the most important were those of the Kutb Sháh dynasty at Golkonda, the 'Ádil Sháhs of Bíjápúr (Vijayapura), and the Nizám Sháhs of Ahmadnagar. Upon these rich States the Mughal emperors often cast longing eyes; but it was reserved for Aurangzíb to be the first to set foot in their prostrate cities.

Akbar was too wise to meddle seriously in Deccan politics. All he wanted was to secure himself against invasion from the south; and with this view he annexed the rugged borderland of Khándésh, and used its capital, Burhánpúr, with the rocky fastness of Asírgarh, as outposts to defend his southern frontier.

He also subdued Berár, and took the fortress of Ahmadnagar. So long as his reign lasted, no harm came of this forward policy: the kings of Bíjápúr and Golkonda were impressed by his boldness, sent embassies to assure him of their admiring goodwill, and consented to pay him tribute. It may be doubted, however, whether he would not have been wiser to draw his scientific frontier at the Narbadá. He set an example which led his successors on to further aggression, and for more than a century the governor of what was known as the *súbah* of the Deccan, which included Burhánpúr and the country round about, was perpetually striving to enlarge his borders at the expense of the dominions of the Nizám, 'Ádil, or Kutb Sháh of the period, with the result that tranquillity was unknown to the inhabitants of the marches. During the reign of Jahángír the struggle went on without advantage to the Mughals; Ahmadnagar was lost and regained; and when Sháh-Jahán ascended the Peacock Throne, the three southern dynasties held most of their old territory, whilst the Mughal province consisted of little more than part of Khándésh and Berár with the fort of Ahmadnagar as a lonely outpost. The new Emperor, who had shown his prowess as a general in the Deccan in his younger days, renewed the contest, extinguished the Nizám Sháh's line, and compelled the kings of Golkonda and Bíjápúr once more to pay homage in the form of a usually unpunctual annual tribute.

Prince Aurangzíb was Viceroy of the Deccan at the

time when these important successes were completed. As has been seen, he was appointed to this, his first official post, on the 10th of May, 1636, when in his eighteenth year. The war was practically over before he arrived on the scene, and all he had to do was to receive the last representative of the Nizám dynasty, and send him to join others of his kindred in the fortress of Gwáliór. The province of the Deccan at this time is described as containing sixty-four forts, fifty-three of which were in the hills, and it was divided into four provinces:—Daulatábád, including Ahmadnagar, its old capital; Telingana; Khándésh; and Berár (capital, Elichpúr). The revenue of the whole was reckoned at five crores, or more than five and a half million pounds. The only addition made during Aurangzíb's first government was the reduction of the territory of Baglána, between Khándésh and the Western Gháts, to the position of a tributary State in the winter of 1637–8. In June, 1643, the Viceroy adopted the profession of a fakír, and was deprived of his office.

Twelve years passed before Aurangzíb returned to the Deccan. The campaigns in Afghánistán had diverted his energies, and the interval had passed peacefully in the south. Sháh-Jahán's officers were busily employed in completing the revenue survey of the Deccan provinces, and the kings of Bíjápúr and Golkonda were quite content to let well alone, so long as the Mughals observed the same maxim. They paid their tribute, as a rule, and in return only asked to be left in peace. This was just what the new Viceroy was least disposed to grant. He had done with his dream of a hermit's contemplative life, and his experience of war in Afghánistán had roused all his inborn passion for conquest. The fact that the Deccan kings were of the heretical sect of the Shí'a, or followers of 'Alí, gave his designs the sacred character of a *Jihád*. From this time to his dying day he never for a moment lost sight of his ambition to recover the empire which had once belonged to Muhammad ibn Taghlak. At last his ambition led him on and on, till for twenty-six years he never set foot in Hindústán, and finally found the grave of his hopes, as of his body, in the land which even his iron will could not subdue.

His first decided step towards the goal he was fated never to reach was an unprovoked attack upon 'Abdallah, the King of Golkonda. The pretext was an internal dispute with which the Mughals had no concern, but it served their purpose. Mír Jumla, the vizier of Golkonda, was by birth a Persian, and a diamond merchant by trade, who had risen to his high office as much by transcendent ability as by fabulous wealth. He was wont to reckon the produce of his diamond mines by the sackful, and used his riches as a serviceable grease to the wheels of success. But he was also a brilliant general, and his campaigns in the Carnatic had brought him fame as well as treasure. In pursuit of both he had shown himself a very scourge of idolatry, and plundered temples and violated idols throughout the peninsula bore witness to his iconoclastic zeal. With such a man Aurangzíb had many grounds of sympathy; and when Mír Jumla fell out with his King, and threw himself upon the protection of the Mughal, it is not surprising that he was welcomed with effusion, and accorded the rank of a 'Commander of 5000.' Having secured this valuable ally, Aurangzíb warmly espoused his cause and set about redressing his wrongs. He sent his eldest son, that 'tender sapling in the garden of success,' Prince Muhammad, to demand justice for Mír Jumla from his former sovereign (Jan., 1656), and took so much pains to disguise his intentions that the astonished King had barely time to escape from his capital, Bhágnagar, afterwards called Haidarábád, to the neighbouring fortress of Golkonda, before his enemies were in the city[1].

Aurangzíb then advanced in person, and laid siege to Golkonda, where he repulsed the King's first sally with a furious charge of the Mughal horse, leading the way on his war-elephant. In vain 'Abdallah sent baskets of gems and gorgeously caparisoned chargers and elephants to appease the besieger: Aurangzíb would listen to no terms; and when the King, as a last resource, begged to be allowed to send his mother as a mediator, the Prince refused to see her. Driven to bay, the King fought hard, but the siege was pressed harder, and when Sháyista Khán came up at the

[1] So Bernier: Kháfí Khán says nothing of this deceit; Catrou on the other hand, *more suo*, dilates upon it with his usual enthusiasm in detraction.

head of the nobles of Málwa to reinforce the Prince, 'Abdallah submitted to the humiliating terms of the conqueror. He consented to engrave Sháh-Jahán's name on his coins, in token of vassalage, to give his daughter in marriage to Aurangzíb's eldest son, with some fortresses to her dowry, and to pay a crore of rupees, or more than a million sterling, in annual tribute to the Emperor. These terms would never have been offered had Aurangzíb had his own way. But Sháh-Jahán was growing jealous of his son's success, and dreaded the consequences of his increased power in the distant provinces of the south; while Dárá, ever envious of his brother's renown, and anxious to curb his ambitious spirit, exerted all his great influence over his aged father to excite his too-ready suspicions of his other sons. Peremptory orders arrived for Aurangzíb to retire from Golkonda, the motive of which the Prince perfectly understood, though he did not feel that the moment for resistance had yet come. But for this interference, Golkonda would have been incorporated in the Mughal Empire in 1656, instead of thirty years later, and much subsequent bloodshed and disorder would have been avoided. As it was, Aurangzíb came to terms with the King on the eve of victory, and withdrew to Aurangábád, which he had made the capital of his province, to nurse his grudge against Dárá, and to plot further schemes of conquest with Mír Jumla.

The result of their deliberations was that Mír Jumla, who now received the title of Mu'azzam Khán, went to Agra, and pleaded the cause of Deccan aggrandizement with Sháh-Jáhan himself. He told the Great Mogul of the wealth and treasures of the south, described the decrepit kingdoms that invited annihilation, and in glowing colours painted the glory that would redound to the name of his most religious Majesty from the extirpation of the effete colony of Portuguese infidels on the Malabar coast. The Mughal, he said, should never rest till his sway was supreme from the Himálayas to Cape Comorin. The crafty Persian did not trust to argument alone: he brought the Emperor a priceless diamond, from the mine of Kollúr on the Kistna, no less a stone than the famous *Koh-i-núr* or 'Peak of Light'; which, after adorning the 'Great Mogul,' was carried away to Persia by Nádir Sháh, brought back to Afghánistán by Ahmad Durrání, and eventually came into the possession of Ranjít Singh, from whom it was transferred to the regalia of England on the annexation of the Punjab in 1849[1]. Fortified by so splendid a gift, Mír Jumla's arguments prevailed, and Sháh-Jahán authorized a further reinforcement of the army of the Deccan with a view to a spirited foreign policy. Dárá fought to the last against this strengthening of his brother's hand, but all he could obtain was the stipulation that Mír Jumla, and not Aurangzíb, should have the command of the new army of aggression, and that the general should leave his family at

[1] The history of this celebrated diamond, and its identity with Mír Jumla's gift, have been conclusively traced by Dr. Ball, in his edition of Tavernier's *Travels*, vol. ii. App. I.

Agra as hostages for his loyalty. The change of command made no difference, as it happened; for Jumla at once joined his troops to Aurangzíb's, in close alliance, and the two proceeded to wrench the castle of Bídar from the possession of 'Ádil Sháh of Bíjápúr. Kaliání and Kulbarga were then taken, and the conquest of Bíjápúr itself seemed imminent, when the serious illness of Sháh-Jahán summoned Aurangzíb away to graver matters [1].

Seven years passed before the troubles in the north, the war of succession, and the initial difficulties of settling his kingdom, left the new Emperor leisure to attend to the affairs of the Deccan. Meanwhile a new power had arisen in the south, a power which sprang from such needy and insignificant beginnings that no one could have foretold its future malignant domination. The Maráthás began to make themselves felt.

This notorious Hindú people inhabited the country lying between the Indian Ocean and the river Warda; their northern boundary was the Satpúra range, and on the west coast they extended as far south as Goa. Their strength lay in the inaccessible fastnesses of the Western Gháts, which climb precipitously to the great plateau that stretches right across the Deccan to the Bay of Bengal.

'The whole of the Gháts and neighbouring mountains often terminate towards the top in a wall of smooth rock, the highest points of which, as well as detached portions on

[1] See above, p. 35.

insulated hills, form natural fortresses, where the only labour required is to get access to the level space, which generally lies on the summit. Various princes at different times have profited by these positions. They have cut flights of steps or winding roads up the rocks, fortified the entrance with a succession of gateways, and erected towers to command the approaches; and then studded the whole region about the Ghâts and their branches with forts, which, but for frequent experience, would be deemed impregnable[1].'

Between the Ghâts and the sea lies the narrow strip of rugged country called the Konkan. Here deep valleys and torrent-beds lead from the rocks and forests of the mountain ridge to the fertile plains of the humid tract near the sea, where the torrents merge in sandy creeks among thickets of mangroves.

'The broken and contorted land, writhing from the rugged and indented sea-margin, shoots aloft in steep and terrific cliffs and craggy summits, whose beauty and majesty must be seen to be understood. Magnificent forests clothe these elevations, and spread far down into the wild country below, and extend their mysterious and treacherous shade for many a mile along the table-land above. Impetuous torrents leap from the mountain sides, rive, in their headlong career sea-ward, the uneven and craggy surface of the coastland; and the hollow *nullas* of the dry season are, on the approach of rain, .transformed in a few hours into deep, furious, and impassable cataracts. The thunderstorms of these regions are terrific: the deluges of rain, violent, copious, and frequent, beyond all comparison elsewhere in India. Roads throughout the greater part of the country

[1] Elphinstone, *History of India*, 5th ed. (1866), p. 615.

there are none; the character of the ground and the luxuriance of the forest jungles alike preclude them[1].'

The Ghâts and the Konkan were the safe retreats of wild beasts and wiry Maráthás.

These people had never made any mark in history before the reign of Aurangzíb. They had been peaceful, frugal husbandmen, like the mass of the lower orders of Hindús, and had given no trouble to their rulers. Their chiefs, or village headmen, were Súdras, of the lowest of the four castes, like their people, though they pretended to trace their pedigree to the Rájputs, and thus connect themselves with the noble caste of Kshatriyas. In the silent times of peace, the Maráthás enjoyed the happiness of the nation that has no history. War brought out their dormant capacities, and their daggers soon cut their name deep in the annals of India.

'They are small, sturdy men,' says Elphinstone, 'well made, though not handsome. They are all active, laborious, hardy, and persevering. If they have none of the pride and dignity of the Rájputs, they have none of their indolence or their want of worldly wisdom. A Rájput warrior, as long as he does not dishonour his race, seems almost indifferent to the result of any contest he is engaged in. A Maráthá thinks of nothing *but* the result, and cares little for the means, if he can attain his object. For this purpose he will strain his wits, renounce his pleasures, and hazard his person; but he has not a conception of sacrificing his life, or even his

[1] Sidney Owen, *India on the Eve of the British Conquest* (1872), p. 22. Dr. Fryer has given a vivid account of his ascent of the Ghâts in his *New Account of India* (1698), Letter III, ch. iv.

interest, for a point of honour. This difference of sentiment effects the outward appearance of the two nations: there is something noble in the carriage even of an ordinary Rájput, and something vulgar in that of the most distinguished Maráthá.'

The vulgar Maráthá, nevertheless, gave more trouble to the rulers of Hindústán, whether Mughal or English, than even the proud dynasties of the Rájputs. The King of Bíjápúr was responsible for the disastrous policy of educating this hardy race for their career of rapine. They formed a large proportion of his subjects, and their language, a peculiar offshoot of Sanskrit, became the official script of the revenue department of his kingdom. Gradually they came to be employed in his army, first in garrison duty, and then in the light cavalry, a branch of service for which they displayed extraordinary aptitude. Some of them rose to offices of some importance at Bíjápúr and Golkonda.. One of the most distinguished of these officers, Sháhjí Bhósla, governor of Poona and Bangalore, was the father of Sivají, the founder of the Maráthá power.

CHAPTER X

Sivají the Maráthá

Sivají was born in May, 1627, and was thus eight years younger than his great adversary Aurangzíb. He was brought up at his father's jágír of Poona, where he was noted for his courage and shrewdness, while 'for craft and trickery he was reckoned a sharp son of the Devil, the Father of Fraud.' He mixed with the wild highlanders of the neighbouring Gháts, and listening to their native ballads and tales of adventure, soon fell in love with their free and reckless mode of life. If he did not join them in their robber raids, at least he hunted through their country, and learnt every turn and path of the Gháts. He found that the hill forts were utterly neglected or miserably garrisoned by the Bíjápúr government, and he resolved upon seizing them, and inaugurating an era of brigandage on a heroic scale. He began by surprising the fort of Tórna, some twenty miles from Poona, and after adding fortress to fortress at the expense of the Bíjápúr kingdom, without attracting much notice, crowned his iniquity in 1648 by making a convoy of royal treasure 'bail up,' and by occupying the whole of the northern Konkan. A few years later he caused the governor of the more southern region of the Gháts to be assassinated, annexed the whole territory, captured the existing forts, and built new strongholds. Like Albuquerque, but with better reason, he posed as the protector of the Hindús against the Musalmáns, whom he really hated with a righteous hatred; and his policy and his superstitious piety alike recommended him to the people, and, in spite of his heavy blackmail, secured their adhesion.

So far Sivají had confined his depredations to the dominions of the King of Bíjápúr. The Mughal territory had been uniformly respected, and in 1649 the Maráthá had shown his political sagacity, and prevented active retaliation on the part of the 'Ádil Sháh, by actually offering his services to Sháh-Jahán, who had been pleased to appoint him to the rank of a 'Mansabdár of 5000.' The freebooter fell indeed under the temptation set before him by the war between Aurangzíb and the Deccan Kings in 1656, and profited by the preoccupation of both sides to make a raid upon Junír. But Aurangzíb's successes soon convinced him that he had made a false move, and he hastened to offer his apologies, which were accepted. Aurangzíb was then marching north to secure his crown, and could not pause to chastise a ridiculously insignificant marauder.

During the years of civil war and ensuing reorganization in Hindústán, Sivají made the best of his opportunities. The young king Sikandar, who had lately succeeded to the throne of Bíjápúr, in vain sought to quell the audacious rebel. An expedition sent against him about 1658 was doomed to ignominious failure, and its commander met a treacherous fate. Sivají knew better than to meet a powerful army in the field; he understood the precise point where courage must give place to cunning, and in dealing with a Muslim foe he had no scruples of honour. When Afzal Khán advanced to the forts and forests of the Gháts at the head of a strong force, the Maráthá hastened to humble himself and tender his profuse apologies, and the better to show his submissive spirit he begged for a private audience, man to man, with the general. The story is typical of the method by which the Maráthás acquired their extraordinary ascendency. Afzal Khán, completely deluded by Sivají's protestations, and mollified by his presents, consented to the interview. Sure of his enemy's good faith, he went unarmed to the rendezvous below the Maráthá fortress, and leaving his attendants a long bowshot behind, advanced to meet the suppliant. Sivají was seen descending from the fort, alone, cringing and crouching in abject fear. Every few steps he paused and quavered forth a trembling confession of his offences against the King his lord. The frightened creature dared not come near till Afzal Khán had sent his palankin bearers to a distance, and stood quite solitary in the forest clearing. The soldier had no fear of the puny quaking figure that came weeping to his feet. He raised him up, and was about to embrace him round the shoulder in the friendly oriental way, when he was suddenly clutched with fingers of steel. The Maráthá's hands were armed with 'tiger's claws'—steel nails as sharp as razors—and his embrace was as deadly as the Scottish 'Maiden's.' Afzal died without a groan. Then the Maráthá trumpet sounded the attack, and from every rock and tree armed ruffians fell upon the Bíjápúrís, who were awaiting the return of their general in careless security. There was no time to think of fighting, it was a case of *sauve qui peut.* They found they had to deal with a lenient foe, however. Sivají had gained his object, and he never indulged in useless bloodshed. He offered quarter, and gained the subdued troopers over to his own standard. It was enough for him to have secured all the baggage, stores, treasure, horses, and elephants of the enemy, without slaking an unprofitable thirst for blood.

Once more the forces of Bíjápúr came out to crush him, and again they retreated in confusion. After this the Deccan sovereign left him unmolested to gather fresh recruits, build new forts, and plunder as he pleased. His brigandage was colossal, but it was conducted under strict rules. He seized caravans and convoys and appropriated their treasure, but he permitted no sacrilege to mosques and no dishonouring of women. If a Korán were taken, he gave it reverently to some Muhammadan. If women were captured, he protected them till they were ransomed. There was nothing of the libertine or brute about Sivají. In the appropriation of booty, however, he was inexorable. Common goods belonged to the finder, but treasure, gold, silver, gems, and satins, must be surrendered untouched to the State[1].

Sivají's rule now extended on the sea coast from Kalyiní in the north to the neighbourhood of Portuguese Goa, a distance of over 250 miles; east of the Gháts it reached from Poona down to Mirich on the Kistna; and its breadth in some parts was as much as 100 miles. It was not a vast dominion, but it supported an army of over 50,000 men, and it had been built up with incredible patience and daring. Like the tiger of his own highland forests, Sivají had crouched and waited until the moment came for the deadly spring. He owed his success as much to feline cunning as to boldness in attack.

He was freed from anxiety on the score of his eastern neighbour the King of Bíjápúr, whose lands he had plundered at his will, and he now longed for fresh fields of rapine. The Hindús had become his friends, or bought his favour, and offered few occasions for pillage. He therefore turned to the Mughal territory to the north. Hitherto he had been careful to avoid giving offence to his adopted suzerain, but now he felt himself strong enough to risk a quarrel. His irrepressible thirst for plunder found ample exercise in the Mughal districts, and though he deprecated an assault upon the capital, lest he should provoke the Emperor to a war of extermination, he pushed

[1] Kháfi Khán, *l. c.*, vol. vii. pp. 260–1.

his raids almost to the gates of the 'Throne-City,' Aurangábád, which was now the metropolis of the Mughal power in the Deccan. Aurangzíb's uncle, Sháyista Khán, then Viceroy of the Deccan, was ordered to put a stop to these disturbances, and accordingly proceeded, in 1660, to occupy the Maráthá country. He found that the task of putting down the robbers was not so easy as it looked, even with the best troops in India at his back. Every fort had to be reduced by siege, and the defence was heroic. A typical instance may be read in Kháfí Khán's description of the attack on the stronghold of Chákna, one of Sivají's chief forts:—

'Then the royal armies marched to the fort of Chákna, and after examining its bastions and walls, they opened trenches, erected batteries, threw up intrenchments round their own position, and began to drive mines under the fort. Thus having invested the place, they used their best efforts to reduce it. The rains in that country last nearly five months, so that people cannot put their heads out of their houses. The heavy masses of clouds change day into night, so that lamps are often needed, for without them one man cannot see another man of a party. But for all the muskets were rendered useless, the powder spoilt, and the bows bereft of their strings, the siege was vigorously pressed, and the walls of the fortress were breached by the fire of the guns. The garrison were hard pressed and troubled, but on dark nights they sallied forth into the trenches and fought with surprising boldness. Sometimes the forces of the freebooter on the outside combined with those inside in making a simultaneous attack in broad daylight, and placed the trenches in great danger. After the siege had lasted fifty or sixty days, a bastion which had been mined was blown up, and stones, bricks, and men flew into the air like pigeons. The brave soldiers of Islám, trusting in God, and placing their shields before them, rushed to the assault and fought with great determination. But the infidels had thrown up a barrier of earth inside the fortress, and had made intrenchments and plans of defence in many parts. All the day passed in fighting, and many of the assailants were killed. But the brave warriors disdained to retreat, and passed the night without food or rest amid the ruins and the blood. As soon as the sun rose, they renewed their attacks, and after putting many of the garrison to the sword, by dint of great exertion and determination they carried the place. The survivors of the garrison retired into the citadel. In this assault 300 of the royal army were slain, besides sappers and others engaged in the work of the siege. Six or seven hundred horse and foot were wounded by stones and bullets, arrows and swords.'

Eventually the citadel surrendered, and Chákna was re-christened 'Islámábád': but assaults and sieges like this cost more than the conquest was worth. Even when the Mughals seemed to have brought the northern part of the Maráthá country under control, and Sivají had buried himself in the hills, a fresh outrage dispelled the illusion. Sháyista Khán was carousing one night in fancied security in his winter quarters at Poona. Suddenly the sounds of slaughter broke upon the ears of the midnight banqueters, who were regaling themselves after the day's fast, for it was the month of Ramazán. The Maráthás were butchering Sháyista's household. They got into the guard-house, and killed every one they found on his pillow, crying, 'This is how they keep watch!' Then they beat the Mughal drums so that nobody could hear his own voice. Sháyista's son was killed in the scuffle, and the general himself was dragged away by some of his faithful slave girls, and with difficulty escaped by a window.

This happened in 1663, after the Mughal army had been occupied for three years in subduing the robbers. The prospect was not encouraging, and to make matters worse the Mughal general laid the blame of the midnight surprise upon the treachery of his Rájput colleague Jaswant Singh. The Rája had played the traitor before: he had tried to desert to Shujá' on the eve of the most decisive battle in Bengal; he had pledged himself to Dárá, and then thrown the unfortunate Prince over for Aurangzíb; and he was suspected of being peculiarly susceptible to monetary arguments. Nothing, however, was proved against him in the Poona affair, and Aurangzíb found his military science and his gallant following of Rájputs too valuable to be lightly discarded. Accordingly, Sháyista was recalled and transferred to Bengal[1], and Prince Mu'azzam, the Emperor's second son, was appointed to the command in the Deccan, with the Rája Jaswant Singh as his colleague. Sivají celebrated the occasion by sacking Súrat for (Fryer says) forty days (Jan.—Feb. 1664): Sir George Oxindon indeed repulsed him from the English factory with much credit, but he carried off a splendid booty from the

[1] See p. 117. He died in Bengal in 1694, aged 93.

city. Nothing more outrageous in the eyes of a good Muslim could be conceived than this insult to Súrat, the 'Gate of the Pilgrimage,' until the sacrilege was eclipsed by the fleet which Sivají fitted out at forts which he had built on the coast, for the express purpose of intercepting Mughal ships, many of which were full of pilgrims on their way to or from the Holy City of Mecca. It seemed as though there were no limits to the audacity of this upstart robber, who, now that his father was dead, presumed to style himself Rája, low caste Maráthá though he was, and to coin money as an independent sovereign.

A fresh change of generals was tried. Jaswant Singh's previous record justified the suspicion that he had turned a blind eye to the doings of his fellow Hindús, the violators of Súrat. He was superseded, and Rája Jai Singh and Dilír Khán were appointed joint-commanders in the Deccan. Aurangzíb never trusted one man to act alone; a colleague was always sent as a check upon him; and the divided command generally produced vacillating half-hearted action. In the present instance, however, Jai Singh and his colleague appear to have displayed commendable energy. Five months they spent in taking forts and devastating the country, and at length Sivají, driven to earth, opened negotiations with Jai Singh, which ended in an extraordinary sensation: the Maráthá chief not only agreed to surrender the majority of his strongholds, and to become once more the vassal of the Emperor, but actually went to Delhi and appeared in person at the Court of the Great Mogul, to do homage to his suzerain for no less a feof than the Viceroyalty of the Deccan. No more amazing apparition than this sturdy little 'mountain rat' among the stately grandeur of a gorgeous Court could be imagined.

The visit was not a success. Aurangzíb clearly did not understand the man he had to deal with, and showed a curious lack of political sagacity in his reception of the Maráthá. No prince or general in all India could render the Emperor such aid in his designs against the Deccan kingdoms as the rude highlander who had at last come to his feet. A good many points might well be stretched to secure so valuable an ally. But Aurangzíb was a bigot, and inclined to be fastidious in some things. He could not forget that Sivají was a fanatical Hindú, and a vulgar brigand to boot. He set himself the task of showing the Maráthá his real place, and, far from recognizing him as Viceroy of the Deccan, let him stand unnoticed among third rank officers in the splendid assembly that daily gathered before the throne in the great Hall of Audience[1]. Deeply

[1] There is some mystery about this interview. Kháfí Khán says, with little probability, that Aurangzíb was not aware of the lavish promises which had been made to Sivají in his name by Jai Singh. Bernier and Fryer explain Aurangzíb's coldness by the clamour of the women, who, like Sháyista's wife, had lost their sons by the hands of the Maráthás. The risk of assassination by the injured relatives of his victims may well have given Sivají a motive for escape from Delhi, but the vengeful appeals of the women could not have dictated Aurangzíb's policy. He never budged an inch from

affronted, the little Maráthá, pale and sick with shame and fury, quitted the presence without taking ceremonious leave. Instead of securing an important ally, Aurangzíb had made an implacable enemy.

He soon realized his mistake when Sivají, after escaping, concealed in a hamper, from the guards who watched his house, resumed his old sway in the Gháts at the close of 1666, nine months after he had set forth on his unlucky visit to Court. He found that the Mughals had almost abandoned the forts in the Gháts, in order to prosecute a fruitless siege of Bíjápúr, and he immediately re-occupied all his old posts of vantage. No punishment followed upon this act of defiance, for Jaswant Singh, the friend of Hindús and affable pocketer of bribes, once more commanded in the Deccan, and the result of his mediation was a fresh treaty, by which Sivají was acknowledged as a Rája, and permitted to enjoy a large amount of territory together with a new jágír in Berár. The kings of Bíjápúr and Golkonda hastened to follow the amicable lead of the Mughal, and purchased their immunity from the Maráthás by paying an annual tribute. Deprived of the excitements of war and brigandage, Sivají fixed his capital in the lofty crag of Ráhirí,

his set purpose to gratify a woman's wish. The rumour that he connived at Sivají's escape, as mentioned by Fryer, in order to make a friend of the man whose life he thus saved, is improbable. Aurangzíb certainly believed that he had more to gain by Sivají's death than by his friendship, which he despised ; and subsequent events showed that the Maráthá did not consider himself at all beholden to the Emperor for his safety.

afterwards Ráígarh, due east of Jinjara, and devoted himself to the consolidation of his dominion. His army was admirably organized and officered, and the men were highly paid, not by feudal chiefs, but by the government, while all treasure trove in their raids had to be surrendered to the State. His civil officials were educated Bráhmans, since the Maráthás were illiterate. Economy in the army and government, and justice and honesty in the local administration, characterized the strict and able rule of this remarkable man.

Aurangzíb's brief attempt at conciliation—if indeed it were such—was soon exchanged for open hostility. He had, perhaps, employed Jaswant Singh in the hope of again luring Sivají into his power; in any case the plot had failed. Henceforth he recognized the deadly enemy he had made by his impolitic hauteur at Delhi. The Maráthá, for his part, was nothing loth to resume his old depredations. He recovered most of his old forts, sacked Súrat a second time in 1671, sent his nimble horsemen on raids into Khándésh, even defeated a Mughal army in the open field, brought all the southern Konkan—except the ports and territory held by the English, Portuguese, and Abyssinians—under his sway, and began to levy the famous Maráthá *chauth* or blackmail, amounting to one-fourth of the revenue of each place, as the price of immunity from brigandage. He even carried his ravages as far north as Baróch, where the Maráthás set an ominous precedent by crossing the Narbadá

(1675). Then he turned to his father's old jágír in the south, which extended as far as Tanjore, and was now held for the King of Bíjápúr by Sivají's younger brother. After forming an alliance with the King of Golkonda, who was jealous of the predominance of Bíjápúr, and after visiting him at the head of 30,000 horsemen and 40,000 foot, Sivají marched south to conquer the outlying possessions of the common enemy, and to bring his brother to a sense of fraternal duty. He passed close to Madras in 1677, captured Jinjí (600 miles from the Konkan) and Vellór and Ární, and took possession of all his father's estates, though he afterwards shared the revenue with his brother. On his return to the Gháts, after an absence of eighteen months, he compelled the Mughals to raise the siege of Bíjápúr, in return for large cessions on the part of the besieged government. Just as he was meditating still greater aggrandizement, a sudden illness put an end to his extraordinary career in 1680, when he was not quite fifty-three years of age. The date of his death is found in the words *Káfir be-jahannam raft*, 'The Infidel went to Hell[1].'

'Though the son of a powerful chief, he had begun life as a daring and artful captain of banditti, had ripened into a skilful general and an able statesman, and left a character which has never since been equalled or approached by any of his countrymen. The distracted state of the neighbouring

[1] Kháfí Khán is proud to be the discoverer of this chronogram. It is, of course, to be interpreted by the numerical values of the consonants: K 20, Alif 1, F 80, R 200, B 2, J 3, H 5, N N 50, 50, R 200, F 80, T 400 = 1091 A. H. (1680).

countries presented openings by which an inferior leader might have profited; but it required a genius like his to avail himself as he did of the mistakes of Aurangzíb, by kindling a zeal for religion, and, through that, a national spirit among the Maráthás. It was by these feelings that his government was upheld after it had passed into feeble hands, and was kept together, in spite of numerous internal disorders, until it had established its supremacy over the greater part of India. Though a predatory war, such as he conducted, must necessarily inflict extensive misery, his enemies bear witness to his anxiety to mitigate the evils of it by humane regulations, which were strictly enforced. His devotion latterly degenerated into extravagances of superstition and austerity, but seems never to have obscured his talents or soured his temper[1].'

'Sivají always strove to maintain the honour of the people in his territories,' says a Muhammadan historian. 'He persisted in rebellion, plundering caravans, and troubling mankind. But he was absolutely guiltless of baser sins, and was scrupulous of the honour of women and children of the Muslims when they fell into his hands.' Aurangzíb himself admitted that his foe was 'a great captain'; and added 'My armies have been employed against him for nineteen years, and nevertheless his State has been always increasing.'

[1] Elphinstone, *History of India*, 5th ed. (1866), p. 647.

CHAPTER XI

The Fall of Golkonda

Aurangzíb had been badly served by his generals in the Deccan: but the fault was his own. His morbid distrust had thwarted their efforts; the command had been divided between jealous rivals; the forces at their disposal had been insufficient to crush Sivají or subdue the southern kings; and the commanders had been too frequently superseded to permit of connected and prolonged energy. It is possible that the languid progress of his arms in the Deccan was not wholly undesigned by the Emperor. He may have intended to give the rival forces in the south time to destroy each other, and anticipated an easy triumph over a disorganized and exhausted enemy. So far as the two kingdoms of Bíjápúr and Golkonda were concerned, his forecast was accurate enough. Their armies seem to have melted away; they had fallen so low as to pay blackmail to the Maráthás: Golkonda had already grovelled before the Mughals, and it was only owing to the interference of Sivají that Bíjápúr had not become a Mughal city in 1679. But the weakening of the old Deccan kingdoms had been procured at the expense of strengthening the Maráthás. Sivají had annexed all the southern territory which his father had lately won for the King of Bíjápúr; he had full possession of the western Gháts and Konkan; and his forts continually sent out armed expeditions to harry the country north and east, wherever the blackmail had not been humbly paid. The 'great Captain', indeed, was dead, but his genius lived in the nation he had created. Aurangzíb could not realize the power of these freebooters. He understood the solid weight of organized states and disciplined armies; but he never estimated the irregular domination of the Maráthás at its true value, until years of fruitless contest had seared the truth upon his mind and spread its witnesses in the starved and butchered corpses of his Grand Army through the length and breadth of the peninsula.

However little he may have appreciated the gravity of the situation which he had suffered to grow up in the Deccan, Aurangzíb saw that the time had come for decisive action. He had by this time come to terms with the Rájputs of Udaipúr[1], and abandoned a vain attempt to subdue the irrepressible tribes of Afghánistán; and, though in neither case could he feel satisfied with the makeshifts he had been obliged to adopt, he felt himself free for a while to dismiss Rájput and Afghán affairs from his mind, and to take the Deccan imbroglio into his own hand. At the close of 1681, Aurangzíb arrived at Burhánpúr, and took

[1] See above, p. 141.

command of the army. He little thought that he should never see Delhi again; that after twenty-six years of stubborn warfare he should die among the ruins of his hopes in the land where he had first held government. Forty-five years before, in 1636, he had come to Khándésh a youthful devotee of seventeen. As a man in the prime of life, he had gone near to conquering the coveted kingdoms (1656). And now at the age of sixty-three he resumed his old work with all his former energy. He could not foresee that a quarter of a century later, a weary old man on the verge of ninety, he would still be there, still fighting the same foe, still enduring the same fatigues and exerting the same iron will, till the worn out frame at last gave way, and the indomitable soul fled to its rest.

The Emperor's first step was to endeavour to strike awe into the Maráthás by sending his sons, the Princes Mu'azzam and A'zam, to scour the country. It was a useless proceeding. The Maráthás offered no opposition, and left their rugged country to punish the invaders. Prince Mu'azzam accordingly marched through the whole Konkan, and laid it waste, and when he reached the end he found that he had hardly a horse fit to carry him, and that his men were marching afoot, half-starving. The enemy had cut down the grass, so that no fodder could be obtained: the Mughal troopers 'had no food but cocoa-nuts, and the grain called kúdún, which acted like poison upon them. Great numbers of men and horses died. Those who escaped death dragged on a half-existence, and with crying and groaning felt as if every breath they drew was their last. There was not a noble who had a horse in his stable fit to use[1].' When they tried to victual the army by sea, the enemy intercepted the corn ships. The rocks and forests of the Ghát country had been quite as destructive to the cavalry as the spears of the Maráthás could have been. Fighting torrents and precipices, and enduring an unhealthy climate and scarcity of food, was an unprofitable business; and the Princes were ordered to converge upon Bíjápúr, whilst Aurangzíb pushed forward to Ahmadnagar.

As soon as the enemy's back was turned, Sivají's son, Sambhájí, swiftly led his active little horsemen behind their flank, and crossing over to Khándésh burned Burhánpúr and set the whole country side in a blaze. Before the Mughals could get at them, they were safe again in their fastnesses in the Gháts. This stroke is typical of the Maráthá method of warfare. They never risked an engagement in the open field unless their numbers made victory a certainty. When the heavy Mughal cavalry attacked them, the hardy little warriors, mounted on wiry steeds as inured to fatigue as themselves, and splendidly broken in for their tactics, would instantly scatter in all directions, and observe the enemy from a neighbouring hill or wood, ready to cut off solitary horsemen, or surprise small parties in ambush; and then, if the pursuers gave up the useless chase, in a moment the Maráthás were upon them, hanging on their flanks,

[1] Kháfí Khán, *l. c.*, vol. vii. p. 314.

despatching stragglers, and firing at close quarters into the unwieldy mass. To fight such people was to do battle with the air or to strike blows upon water: like wind or waves they scattered and bent before the blow, only to close in again the moment the pressure was taken off. They would dash down from their mountain retreats and intercept a rich convoy of treasure; and before the Mughals could get near them they were back in their rocky forts. Even if pursued to their lair and smoked out, so to speak, they only went to some equally convenient and almost inaccessible stronghold to resume their usual trade of plunder, in which they took unfeigned delight. It is true they had no longer a leader of Sivají's capacity, for his son was an idle dissolute sot, whose spasmodic days of daring rapine were separated by long intervals of languid inaction. But the time when a leader was essential was over. Sivají had converted an easy-going race of peasants into a nation of banditti, fired by a universal love of plunder, and inspired by a universal hatred of the Muslim. The Maráthás were no longer the fairly disciplined army that Sivají had organized; they had become independent bands of brigands, each acting for itself, and grasping all that came within reach. But the effect was the same as if they had still formed one force under one leader. Each man fought and trapped and pillaged in the same common cause—the national war against Muhammadan aliens—and their separate efforts produced a sufficiently alarming collective result. Like other brigands, however, they were good to their friends. Those who paid the stipulated blackmail had nothing to fear from their raiding parties. They were consequently popular enough with the country-folk, who regarded them as national heroes, and as their defenders against the inroads of the infidels, and were always eager to keep them informed of the movements of the enemy and to warn them of any approaching danger. It is not too much to say that, except the large cities, and the spots where the Mughal armies were actually encamped, the Deccan was practically under the control of these highland robbers.

A good deal of this must have been apparent to the keen glance of Aurangzíb, as soon as he had come into personal relations with the Maráthás; but he was not to be turned from the course he had set before him. The religious bigotry of the enemy only inflamed his own puritanical zeal, and he was imprudent enough to insist on the strict levying of his poll-tax on Hindús —which had considerably helped the popularity of the Maráthás—in the very country where it was most important to lay aside Muhammadan prejudices. His first step on arriving in the Deccan was to issue stringent orders for the collection of the hated *jizya*. The people and their headmen resisted and rioted in vain. A tried officer was detached with a force of horse and foot to extort the poll-tax and punish the recusants. It is significant that in three months this sagacious officer reported that he had collected the poll-tax of Burhánpúr for the past year (R26,000), and begged the Emperor to appoint some one else to carry on the unpleasant business[1]. Later on a proclamation was issued that no Hindú should ride in a palankin or mount an Arab horse without special permission. The inevitable result of these impolitic measures was to throw the whole Hindú population into the arms of their friends the Maráthás, who indeed exacted a heavy blackmail, but made no invidious distinction of creed in their rough and ready system of taxation.

Aurangzíb's plan seems to have been, first, to cut off the sources of the Maráthá revenue, by exterminating the kingdoms of Golkonda and Bíjápúr, which paid tribute to the brigands; and then to ferret the 'mountain rats' out of their holes. He clearly thought that the two kingdoms formed his real point of attack, and that after their fall it would be easy to deal with the Maráthás. Evidently he did not know his men.

The first part of his programme was the less difficult to carry out. The old Deccan kingdoms were in no condition to offer serious resistance to Aurangzíb's Grand Army. They might have been annexed long before, but for the selfish indolence of the Mughal generals. The truth is, as Bernier[2] shrewdly remarks, that these commanders enjoyed their almost royal dignity so much, while at the head of large armies

[1] Kháfí Khán, *l.c.*, vol. vii. pp. 310, 311.

[2] Bernier was at Golkonda in 1667, and has left on record a singular penetrating survey of the political condition of the Deccan kingdoms and their relations with the Mughals (*Travels*, pp. 191–198).

in a province far distant from the imperial control, that they thought only of keeping their posts, and took very little trouble to bring the enemy to their knees. 'They conduct every operation with languor, and avail themselves of any pretext for the prolongation of war, which is alike the source of their emolument and dignity. It is become a proverbial saying that the Deccan is the bread and support of the soldiers of Hindústán.'

Golkonda was the weaker of the two kingdoms. It had always pushed forward its neighbour Bíjápúr as a buffer to deaden the shock of the Mughal assaults. It had secretly subsidized its neighbour to enable it to defend itself against the Mughals, and at the same time bribed the Imperial officers to attack Bíjápúr rather than itself. In spite of its ingenuity, however, Golkonda had bowed the knee before Aurangzíb in 1656, and had been growing more and more demoralized in the quarter of a century which had rolled by uneasily since then. It was practically a province of the Mughal empire. Its King, Abu-l-Hasan, had never recovered from the shock of that early humiliation. He had become a mere tributary vassal, and had ceased to take any public part in the government of his kingdom. He never appeared in audience, or presided over a court of justice. In 1667 he lived strictly secluded in the fortress of Golkonda, and abandoned himself to debauchery. Meanwhile his metropolis, Haidarábád, was a prey to anarchy and misrule. Relieved from the smallest fear or respect for the King, the nobles tyrannized over the people at their will, and the lower classes would sooner have submitted to Aurangzíb's just governance than continue to endure the oppression of their many masters. Indeed, the rule of the Mughal may almost be said to have been established at Haidarábád from the date of the treaty of 1656, for Aurangzíb's Resident there was accustomed to 'issue his commands, grant passports, menace and ill-treat the people, and in short speak and act with the uncontrolled authority of an absolute sovereign.' Mír Jumla's son, Muhammad Amín Khán, exercised practically royal powers at the principal port, Masulipatan; and Mughals, Dutch, and Portuguese had only to prefer their demands, sure of the fulfilment of the prophecy, 'Ask, and it shall be given unto you.'

It seemed hardly worth while to subdue still further an already prostrate kingdom: but the anarchical state of the government might well invite and even require forcible intervention. When Aurangzíb learnt that two Hindús had possessed themselves of the chief power in Haidarábád, and were oppressing and persecuting the Musalmáns, he felt that the time for intervention had come. A disordered State was an eyesore on his borders; a tributary State where the true believers were persecuted for righteousness' sake was intolerable. Accordingly, in 1684, Prince Mu'azzam was despatched with Khán-Jahán Bahádur Kokaltásh to reform the government of Golkonda. The prince and the general appear to have fallen victims to the indolence which was the besetting sin of Mughal commanders in the Deccan. Mu'azzam was a mild and dutiful son, whose gentle docility laid him perpetually open to the suspicion of designing subtlety. His father had suspected him of ambitions which were wholly foreign to his placid nature, and few princes have won credit for so much devilry as Mu'azzam acquired by the consistent practice of all the innocent virtues. Aurangzíb had not forgotten that his own blameless youth had veiled the fiercest ambition, and his other son, Prince A'zam, was not slow to point the precedent to the case of Mu'azzam. He was 'too good to be true,' evidently. He was certainly too just and humane to be sent to wage a pitiless war. Instead of attacking Haidarábád and Golkonda with the energy which his father expected, the Prince strove in every way to avert hostilities, and then, after some futile skirmishing, for four or five months he remained motionless. It is not surprising to hear that Aurangzíb administered a trenchant reprimand, which 'incensed' the blameless Prince, but induced him at length to fight. Even when he had beaten the enemy and pursued them into their camp, he gave them a truce for the alleged purpose of removing their women to safety, and was rewarded by renewed resistance. He then threw out an imbecile proposal that the dispute should be settled by a combat between two or three heroes on either side, the Horatii and Curiatii of Delhi and Golkonda! This does not seem to have been taken up, and at last the Prince drew near to Haidarábád, where he ought to have been six months before.

On his tardy approach, the greatest terror and confusion prevailed in the city. The Hindús accused the Muhammadans of betraying their country, and the Muhammadan general went over to the Mughals. The King fled to the fortress of Golkonda, and the city was given over to rival bands of rioters, who plundered and raped and destroyed at their pleasure. There was a stampede to Golkonda, and many thousand gentlemen, unable to save their property or find horses, took their wives and children by the hand, and led them, without veils and scantily clothed, to the protection of the fort.

> 'Before break of day, the imperial forces attacked the city, and a frightful scene of plunder and destruction followed, for in every part and road and market there were lacs upon lacs of money, stuffs, carpets, horses, and elephants, belonging to Abu-l-Hasan and his nobles. Words cannot express how many women and children of Musalmáns and Hindús were made prisoners, or how many women of high and low degree were dishonoured. Carpets of great value, which were too heavy to carry, were cut to pieces with swords and daggers, and every bit was struggled for. The Prince appointed officers to prevent the plunder, and they did their best to restrain it, but in vain[1].'

After all these horrors, Prince Mu'azzam, or as he was now styled, Sháh-'Álam ('King of the World') made peace (1685), on the King's agreeing to pay an

[1] Kháfi Khán, *l. c.*, vol. vii. p. 320.

indemnity of about a million and a quarter, to surrender certain districts, and to imprison the two Hindú ministers—who in the meanwhile were murdered by the slaves of the harím. Aurangzíb must have gnashed his teeth when he heard that his son had tamely surrendered the fruits of his victory: but he pretended to approve the terms of peace, whilst privately telling Sháh-'Álam what he thought of him. The Prince was recalled.

Aurangzíb, however, was not, perhaps, sorry to leave Golkonda alone for awhile, as he was now fully occupied with his invasion of Bíjápúr. This kingdom, though more important, and far less accessible, by reason of its fortified mountain passes and the scarcity of forage and water, was in little better case for resistance than its sister State. Its outlying cities had already fallen to the Mughals, and its western districts were in the greedy hands of the Maráthás, who, nevertheless, had been a chief cause why it had not so far succumbed to the imperial attacks. Now that Sivají was dead, this source of protection had vanished, and Prince A'zam was deputed to achieve the long deferred conquest. The Bíjápúrís, however, resorted to their usual tactics · they laid waste all the country round the capital, till the Mughal army was half famished, and they hovered about its flanks and harassed its movements with a pertinacity worthy of Sivají himself. In August, 1685, however, Aurangzíb, appeared upon the scene in person. Under his searching eye the work of intrenching and mining round the six miles of ramparts went on heartily. A close blockade was established, and at last after more than a year's labour the besieged were starved out, and the keys of Bíjápúr were delivered to the Emperor in November, 1686. The old capital of the 'Ádil Sháhs, once full of splendid palaces, became the home of the owl and jackal. It stands yet, a melancholy silent ruin. Its beautiful mosques still raise their minarets above the stone walls, which are even now so inviolate that one might fancy one gazed upon a living city. Within, all is solitude and desolation. The 'Visiapur' which astounded so many travellers by its wealth and magnificence, was trampled under the foot of the Puritan Emperor, and fell to rise no more.

Golkonda soon felt the loss of her protecting sister. In spite of the treaty concluded in 1685, Aurangzíb resolved to make an end of the Kutb Sháh dynasty. His sole justification seems to be that the King had failed to pay the stipulated tribute; but instead of plainly setting forth this ground of complaint, he acted with a dissimulation which was as unnecessary as it was unworthy. Under cover of a pilgrimage to a holy shrine, he marched to Kulbarga, half-way to Golkonda. His agent at Haidarábád was instructed meanwhile to extort the tribute from the King. Abu-l-Hasan collected all the jewels he could lay hands on, and deposited them in baskets at the Mughal Legation by way of security for his debt. Then news came that the Emperor had left Kulbarga and was marching on the capital. His hostile intentions were unmistakable. The King was naturally indignant at the breach of faith, demanded his jewels back, and placed the Mughal Resident under arrest; but on the latter pointing out the inevitable vengeance that would follow any injury offered to Aurangzíb's representative, and proffering his mediation with his master, Abu-l-Hasan restored him to liberty.

The Mughal army was at his gates, and the wretched King knew that his fall was at hand. In vain he sent submissive messages to the Emperor, and laid his humble protestations of obedience at his feet. Aurangzíb's reply was uncompromising:—

'The evil deeds of this wicked man pass the bounds of writing, but to mention one out of a hundred and a little out of much will give some idea of them. He has given the reins of government into the hands of vile tyrannical infidels; oppressed the holy men of Islám; and abandoned himself openly to reckless debauchery and vice, indulging in drunkenness and lewdness day and night. He makes no distinction between infidelity and Islám, tyranny and justice, depravity and devotion. He has waged war on behalf of infidels, and disobeyed the laws of God, which forbid the aiding of the enemies of Islám, by which disobedience he has cast reproach upon the Holy Book in the sight of God and man. Letters of warning and counsel have repeatedly been sent to him by the hands of discreet messengers, but he has paid no heed. Only recently he has sent a lac of pagodas to the wicked Sambhájí. In all this insolence and vice and depravity, he has shown no shame for his infamous offences, and no hope of amendment in this world or the next.'

Seeing that there was no hope of mercy, the King

of Golkonda prepared to die like a soldier. He cast off his sloth and luxury of life, and set about ordering his army and making ready for the siege of his citadel. In January, 1687, the enemy took ground at gunshot range, and the leaguer began. Day by day and week by week the approaches were pushed forward under the command of Ghází-ad-dín Fíróz Jang. Abu-l-Hasan had forty or fifty thousand horse outside the walls which continually harassed the engineers, and the garrison plied their cannon and rockets with deadly effect upon the trenches. The defence was heroic; frequent and deadly were the sallies of the besieged. The fortress was well found in ammunition and provisions, and a ceaseless fire was kept up night and day from the gates and towers and ramparts. Not a day passed without loss to the assailants. At last the lines were pushed up to the fosse, and Aurangzíb himself sewed the first sack that was to be filled with earth and thrown into the ditch. Heavy guns were mounted on earthworks to keep back the defenders, and an attempt was made to scale the walls by night. Some of the besiegers had already gained the ramparts, when a dog gave the alarm, and the garrison speedily despatched the climbers and threw down the ladders. The dog was rewarded with a golden collar.

Meanwhile famine was reducing the Mughal army to extremities. The friends of Golkonda, and especially the Maráthás of 'that hell-dog' Sambhájí, had laid the country waste; the season was dry; and there was a terrible scarcity of rice, grain, and fodder.

Plague broke out in the camp, and many of the soldiers, worn out with hunger and misery, deserted to the enemy. When the rain came at last, it fell in torrents for three days, and washed away much of the entrenchments: upon which the besieged sallied out in force and killed many of the Mughals, and took prisoners. The occasion seemed favourable for overtures of peace. Abu-l-Hasan showed his prisoners the heaps of corn and treasure in the fort, and offered to pay an indemnity, and to supply the besieging army with grain, if the siege were raised. Aurangzíb's answer was full of his old proud inflexible resolve: 'Abu-l-Hasan must come to me with clasped hands, or he shall come bound before me. I will then consider what mercy I can show him.' Forthwith he ordered 50,000 sacks from Berár to fill the moat.

In June the mines were ready to be fired. A feint attack was made to draw off the garrison from the expected breach, and the fuse was applied. The result was disastrous to the Mughals; the defenders had skilfully countermined, and drawn the powder from one mine, and poured water into the others. The only part that exploded was that nearest to the besiegers, who were wounded and buried by the falling stones, and had scarcely recovered from the shock when the garrison were upon them slaying all who were found in the trenches. 'Great wailings and complaints arose from the troops,' and the cannonade from the castle grew hotter as the besiegers' courage waned. Aurangzíb was enraged at the obstinacy of the defence, and commanded an assault to be made under his own eyes.

'Prodigies of valour were exhibited. But a storm of wind and rain arose and obstructed the progress of the assailants, and they were forced to fall back drenched with rain. The garrison again made a sally, took possession of the trenches, spiked the heavy guns, and carried away all that was portable. They pulled out of the moat the logs of wood and the many thousands of bags which had been used to fill it up, and used them to repair the breaches made by the mines[1].'

Where courage and perseverance failed, treason succeeded. Mines and assaults had been vainly tried against the heroic defenders of Golkonda: money and promises at last won the day. Many of the nobles of Golkonda had from time to time gone over to the enemy, and at length only two chiefs remained loyal to the King, 'Abd-ar-Razzák and 'Abdallah Khán. Both had been plied with rich promises by Aurangzíb. 'Abd-ar-Razzák, 'ungracious faithful fellow,' as his friend the historian relates, 'taking no heed of his own interest and life,' showed the Emperor's letter to the men in his bastion, and tore it to shreds before them. He told the spy who brought it to make answer that he would fight to the death, even as they fought who did battle for the blessed Husain at Kerbelá. But his colleague, 'Abdallah Khán, was open to a bribe. He had charge of a postern gate, and admitted the enemy. The Mughals poured into

[1] Kháfí Khán, *l. c.*, vol. vii. p. 331.

the fortress, and raised a shout of triumph. 'Abd-ar-Razzák heard it, and leaping on a barebacked horse, followed by a dozen retainers, galloped to the gate, through which the enemy were rushing in. He threw himself alone into their midst, crying that he would die for Abu-l-Hasan. Covered with blood and reeling in his saddle, he fought his way out, and they found him next day lying senseless under a cocoa-nut tree, with more than seventy wounds.

Meanwhile the King had heard the shouts and groans, and knew that the hour was come. He went into the harím and tried to comfort the women, and then asking their pardon for his faults he bade them farewell, and taking his seat in the audience chamber, waited calmly for his unbidden guests. He would not suffer his dinner hour to be postponed for such a trifle as the Mughal triumph. When the officers of Aurangzíb appeared, he saluted them as became a King, received them courteously, and spoke to them in choice Persian. He then called for his horse and rode with them to Prince A'zam, who presented him to Aurangzíb. The Great Mogul treated him with grave courtesy, as King to King, for the gallantry of his defence of Golkonda atoned for many sins of his licentious past. Then he was sent a prisoner to Daulatábád, where his brother of Bíjápúr was already a captive, and both their dynasties disappear from history. Aurangzíb appropriated some seven millions sterling from the royal property of Golkonda.

The hero of the siege was 'Abd-ar-Razzák. Aurangzíb said that had Abu-l-Hasan possessed but one more servant as loyal as this, the siege might have gone on much longer. He sent a European and a Hindú surgeon to attend to the wounded man, and rejoiced when after sixteen days he at last opened his eyes. He showered favours upon the hero's sons, but nothing could shake the loyalty of the father. Lying on his sick bed, he said that 'no man who had eaten the salt of Abu-l-Hasan could enter the service of Aurangzíb.' Among the universal self-seeking of the Mughal Court, such faithfulness was rare indeed, and no one honoured it more sincerely than the Emperor who had never been disloyal to his standard of duty.

CHAPTER XII

THE RUIN OF AURANGZÍB

WITH the conquest of Golkonda and Bíjápúr, Aurangzíb considered himself master of the Deccan. Yet the direct result of this destruction of the only powers that made for order and some sort of settled government in the peninsula was to strengthen the hands of the Maráthás. The check exercised upon these free-lances by the two Kingdoms may have been weak and hesitating, but it had its effect in somewhat restraining their audacity. Now this check was abolished; the social organization which hung upon the two governments was broken up; and anarchy reigned in its stead. The majority of the vanquished armies naturally joined the Maráthás and adopted the calling of the road. The local officials set themselves up as petty sovereigns, and gave their support to the Maráthás as the party most likely to promote a golden age of plunder. Thus the bulk of the population of the two dissolved States went to swell the power of Sambhájí and his highlanders, and the disastrous results of this revolution in Deccan politics were felt for more than a century. The anarchy which desolated the Deccan was the direct forerunner of the havoc wrought by the Maráthás in Delhi in the time of Sháh-'Álam and Wellesley.

The evil effects of the conquest were not immediately apparent. Aurangzíb's armies seemed to carry all before them, and the work of taking possession of the whole territory of the vanished kingdoms, even as far south as Sháhjí's old government in Mysore, was swiftly accomplished. Sivají's brother was hemmed in at Tanjore, and the Maráthás were everywhere driven away to their mountain forts. To crown these successes, Sambhájí was captured by some enterprising Mughals at a moment of careless self-indulgence. Brought before Aurangzíb, the loathly savage displayed his talents for vituperation and blasphemy to such a degree that he was put to death with circumstances of exceptional barbarity (1689). His brother, Rája Rám, fled to Jinjí in the Carnatic, as remote as possible from the Mughal head-quarters. For the moment, the Maráthá power seemed to have come to an end. The brigands were awed awhile by the commanding personality and irresistible force of the Great Mogul. Had terms with such an enemy been possible or in any degree binding, Aurangzíb might well have accepted some form of tributary homage, and retired to Delhi with all the honours of the war.

But the Emperor was not the man to look back when once his hand was set to the plough. He had accomplished a military occupation not merely of the Deccan, but of the whole peninsula, save the extreme point south of Trichinopoly, and the marginal possessions of the Portuguese and other foreign nations. Military occupation, however, was not enough; he would make the southern provinces an integral part of his settled Empire, as finally and organically a member of it as the Punjáb or Bengal. With this aim he stayed on and on, till a hope and will unquenchable in life were stilled in death. The exasperating struggle lasted seventeen years after the execution of Sambhájí and the capture of his chief stronghold: and at the end success was as far off as ever. 'But it was the will of God that the stock of this turbulent family should not be rooted out of the Deccan, and that King Aurangzíb should spend the rest of his life in the work of repressing them.'

The explanation of this colossal failure is to be found partly in the contrast between the characters of the invaders and the defenders. Had the Mughals been the same hardy warriors that Bábar led from the valleys of the Hindú Kúsh, or had the Rájputs been the loyal protagonists that had so often courted destruction in their devoted service of earlier emperors, the Maráthás would have been allowed but a short shrift. But Aurangzíb had alienated the Rájputs for ever, and they could not be trusted to risk their lives for him in the questionable work of exterminating a people who were Hindús, however inferior in caste and dignity. As for the Mughals, three or four generations of court-life had ruined their ancient manliness. Bábar would have scorned to command such officers as surrounded Aurangzíb in his gigantic camp at Pairampúr. Instead of hardy swordsmen, they had become padded dandies. They wore wadding under their heavy armour, and instead of a plain soldierly bearing they luxuriated in comfortable saddles, and velvet housings, and bells and ornaments on their chargers. They were adorned for a procession, when they should have been in rough campaigning outfit. Their camp was as splendid and luxurious as if they were on guard at the palace at Delhi. The very rank and file grumbled if their tents were not furnished as comfortably as in quarters at Agra, and their requirements attracted an immense crowd of camp followers, twenty times as numerous as the effective strength. An eye-witness describes Aurangzíb's camp at Galgala in 1695 as enormous: the royal tents alone occupied a circuit of three miles, defended all round with palisades and ditches and 500 falconets:—

'I was told,' he says, 'that the forces in this camp amounted to 60,000 horse and 100,000 on foot, for whose baggage there were 50,000 camels and 3000 elephants; but that the sutlers, merchants and artificers were much more numerous, the whole camp being a moving city containing five millions of souls, and abounding not only in provisions, but in all things that could be desired. There were 250 bazars or markets, every Amír or general having one to serve his men. In short the whole camp was thirty miles about[1].'

[1] Dr. J. F. Gemelli Careri, *Voyage Round the World*, Churchill Collection of Voyages and Travels, vol. iv. p. 221 (1745). He adds that the total army amounted to 300,000 horse and 400,000 foot. He

So vast a host was like a plague of locusts in a country: it devoured everything; and though at times it was richly provisioned, at others the Maráthás cut off communications with the base of supplies in the north, and a famine speedily ensued.

The effeminacy of the Mughal soldiers was encouraged by the dilatory tactics of their generals. The best of all Aurangzíb's officers, Zú-l-Fikár, held treasonable parley with the enemy and intentionally delayed a siege, in the expectation that the aged Emperor would die at any moment and leave him in command of the troops. Such generals and such soldiers were no match for the hardy Maráthás, who were inspired to a man with a burning desire to extirpate the Musalmáns and plunder everything they possessed. The Mughals had numbers and weight; in a pitched battle they were almost always successful, and their sieges, skilfully conducted, were invariably crowned with the capture of the fort. But these forts were innumerable; and each demanded months of labour before it would surrender; and in an Indian climate there are not many consecutive months in which siege operations can be carried on without severe hardships. We constantly hear of marches during the height of the rains, the Emperor leading the way in his uncomplaining stoical fashion, and many of the nobles trudging on foot through the mud. In a single campaign no less than 4000 miles

doubtless fell into the common error of including a large proportion of camp followers in the infantry.

were covered, with immense loss in elephants, horses, and camels. Against such hardships the effeminate soldiers rebelled. They were continually crying for 'the flesh-pots of Egypt,' the comfortable tents and cookery of their cantonment at Bairampúr.

The Maráthás, on the other hand, cared nothing for luxuries: hard work and hard fare were their accustomed diet, and a cake of millet sufficed them for a meal, with perhaps an onion for 'point.' They defended a fort to the last, and then defended another fort. They were pursued from place to place, but were never daunted, and they filled up the intervals of sieges by harassing the Mughal armies, stopping convoys of supplies, and laying the country waste in the path of the enemy. There was no bringing them to a decisive engagement. It was one long series of petty victories followed by larger losses.

To narrate the events of the guerilla warfare, which filled the whole twenty years which elapsed between the conquest of Golkonda and the death of Aurangzíb, would be to write a catalogue of mountain sieges and an inventory of raids. Nothing was gained that was worth the labour; the Maráthás became increasingly objects of dread to the demoralized Mughal army; and the country, exasperated by the sufferings of a prolonged occupation by an alien and licentious soldiery, became more and more devoted to the cause of the intrepid bandits, which they identified as their own. An extract from the Muhammadan historian, Kháfí Khán, who is loth to record disaster to his sovereign's arms, will give a sufficient idea of the state of the war in 1702. At this time Tárá Báí, the widow of Rám Rája, was queen-regent of the Maráthás, as Sambhájí's son was a captive in the hands of Aurangzíb. Tárá Báí deserves a place among the great women of history:—

'She took vigorous measures for ravaging the imperial territory, and sent armies to plunder the six provinces of the Deccan as far as Sironj, Mandisor, and Málwa. She won the hearts of her officers, and for all the struggles and schemes, the campaigns and sieges of Aurangzíb, up to the end of his reign, the power of the Maráthás increased day by day. By hard fighting, by the expenditure of the vast treasures accumulated by Sháh-Jahán, and by the sacrifice of many thousands of men, he had penetrated into their wretched country, had subdued their lofty forts, and had driven them from house and home; still their daring increased, and they penetrated into the old territories of the imperial throne, plundering and destroying wherever they went. . . . Whenever the commander of the army hears of a large caravan, he takes six or seven thousand men and goes to plunder it. If the collector cannot levy the *chauth*, the general destroys the towns. The head men of the villages, abetted by the Maráthás, make their own terms with the imperial revenue-officers. They attack and destroy the country as far as the borders of Ahmadábád and the districts of Málwa, and spread their devastations through the provinces of the Deccan to the environs of Ujjain. They fall upon and plunder caravans within ten or twelve *kos* of the imperial camp, and have even had the hardihood to attack the royal treasure [1].'

[1] See Elliot and Dowson, vol. vii. p. 375.

They carried off the imperial elephants within hail of the cantonments, and even shut the Emperor up in his own trenches, so that 'not a single person durst venture out of the camp[1].'

The marvellous thing about this wearisome campaign of twenty years is the way in which the brave old Emperor endured its many hardships and disappointments.

'He was nearly sixty-five when he crossed the Narbada to begin on this long war, and had attained his eighty-first year before he quitted his cantonment at Bairampúr [to make his last grand sweep over the Maráthá country]. The fatigues of marches and sieges were little suited to such an age; and in spite of the display of luxury in his camp equipage, he suffered hardships that would have tried the constitution of a younger man. While he was yet at Bairampúr, a sudden flood of the Bhíma overwhelmed his cantonment in the darkness of the night, and during the violence of one of those falls of rain which are only seen in tropical climates: a great portion of the cantonment was swept away, and the rest laid under water; the alarm and confusion increased the evil: 12,000 persons are said to have perished, and horses, camels, and cattle without number. The Emperor himself was in danger, the inundation rising over the elevated spot which he occupied, when it was arrested (as his courtiers averred) by the efficacy of his prayers. A similar disaster was produced by the descent of a torrent during the siege of Parlí; and, indeed, the storms of that inclement region must have exposed him to many sufferings during the numerous rainy seasons he spent within it. The impassable streams, the flooded valleys, the miry bottoms, and narrow ways, caused

[1] Bundela officer's narrative, in Scott's *Deccan*, pp. 109, 116.

still greater difficulties when he was in motion; compelled him to halt where no provisions were to be had; and were so destructive to his cattle as sometimes entirely to cripple his army. The violent heats, in tents, and during marches, were distressing at other seasons, and often rendered overpowering by the failure of water: general famines and pestilences came more than once, in addition to the scarcity and sickness to which his own camp was often liable; and all was aggravated by the accounts of the havoc and destruction committed by the enemy in the countries beyond the reach of these visitations[1].'

In the midst of these manifold discouragements Aurangzíb displayed all his ancient energy. It was he who planned every campaign, issued all the general orders, selected the points for attack and the lines of entrenchment, and controlled every movement of his various divisions in the Deccan. He conducted many of the sieges in person, and when a mine exploded on the besiegers at Sattára, in 1699, and general despondency fell on the army, the octogenarian mounted his horse and rode to the scene of disaster 'as if in search of death.' He piled the bodies of the dead into a human ravelin, and was with difficulty prevented from leading the assault himself. He was still the man who chained his elephant at the battle of Samúgarh. Nor was his energy confined to the overwhelming anxieties of the war. His orders extended to affairs in Afghánistán, and disturbances at Agra; he even thought of retaking Kandahár. Not an

[1] Elphinstone (1866), pp. 665, 666.

officer, not a government clerk, was appointed without his knowledge, and the conduct of the whole official staff was vigilantly scrutinized with the aid of an army of spies.

We are fortunate in possessing a portrait[1] of Aurangzíb, as he appeared in the midst of his Deccan campaigns. On Monday the 21st of March, 1695, Dr. Gemelli Careri was admitted to an audience of the Emperor in his quarters, called 'Gulalbar,' at the camp of Galgala. He saw an old man with a white beard, trimmed round, contrasting vividly with his olive skin; 'he was of low stature, with a large nose; slender and stooping with age.' Sitting upon rich carpets, and leaning against gold-embroidered cushions, he received the Neapolitan courteously, asked his business in the camp, and, being told of Careri's travels in Turkey, made inquiries about the war then raging between the Sultan and the princes of Hungary. The doctor saw him again at the public audience in the great tent within a court enclosed by screens of painted calico. The Mughal appeared leaning on a crutched staff, preceded by several nobles. He was simply attired in a white robe, tied under the right arm, with a silk sash, from which his dagger hung. On his head was a white turban bound with a gold web, 'on which an emeraud of a vast bigness appear'd amidst four little ones. His shoes were after the Moorish fashion, and his legs naked without

[1] Gemelli Careri, *Voyage Round the World*, Churchill Coll., vol. iv. pp. 222, 223.

hose.' He took his seat upon a square gilt throne raised two steps above the dais, inclosed with silver banisters; three brocaded pillows formed the sides and back, and in front was a little silver footstool. Over his head a servant held a green umbrella to keep off the sun, whilst two others whisked the flies away with long white horsetails. 'When he was seated they gave him his scimitar and buckler, which he laid down on his left side within the throne. Then he made a sign with his hand for those that had business to draw near; who being come up, two secretaries, standing, took their petitions, which they delivered to the King, telling him the contents. I admir'd to see him indorse them with his own hand, without spectacles, and by his cheerful smiling countenance seem to be pleased with the employment.'

One likes to think of Aurangzíb as the Neapolitan doctor saw him, simply dignified, cheerfully busy, leading his austere life of devotion and asceticism in the midst of his great camp in the Deccan. It is a wonderful picture of the vigorous old age of one who allowed no faculty of his active mind to rust, no spring of his spare frame to relax. But behind that serene mask lay a gloomy, lonely soul. It was the tragical fate of the Mughal Emperor to live and die alone. Solitary state was the heritage of his rank, and his natural bent of mind widened the breach that severed him from those around him. The fate of Sháh-Jahán preyed upon his mind. He was wont to remind his sons that he was not one to be treated as he had used his own father. His eldest son had paid the penalty of his brief and flighty treason by a life-long captivity; and Aurangzíb had early impressed the lesson upon the second brother. 'The art of reigning,' he told Mu'azzam, 'is so delicate, that a king must be jealous of his own shadow. Be wise, or a fate like your brother's will befall you also.' Mu'azzam had been docility personified, but his father's suspicion had been aroused more than once, and his next brother A'zam had shown a strictly Mughal spirit in fanning the sombre glow, till the exemplary heir was thrown into prison, where he endured a rigorous captivity for seven years (1687–94). On his release, A'zam became in turn the object of jealousy, perhaps with better reason, and a curious story is told of the way in which the Emperor convinced his son of the futility of conspiracy:—

'Having imbibed a suspicion that this Prince was meditating independence, he sent for him to Court; and as the Prince made excuses and showed alarm, he offered to meet him slightly attended on a hunting-party. A'zam on this set out, and Aurangzíb secretly surrounded the place of meeting with chosen troops: as the Prince got more and more within his toils, the old Emperor found a succession of pretences for requiring him gradually to diminish the number of his attendants, until, when they reached the place where his father was, they were reduced to three persons. As nobody offered to undertake the duty, he was obliged to leave two of his companions to hold his horses; and he and the remaining attendant were disarmed before they were admitted to the royal presence. On this he gave himself up for lost, and had no doubt that he was doomed to a long or perpetual imprisonment. But when he was introduced to his father, he was received with an affectionate embrace: Aurangzíb, who was prepared for shooting, gave his loaded gun for him to hold, and then led him into a retired tent, where he showed him a curious family sword, and put it naked into his hand that he might examine it; after which he threw open his vest, on pretence of heat, but really to show that he had no hidden armour. After this display of confidence, he loaded A'zam with presents, and at last said he had better think of retiring, or his people would be alarmed at his detention. This advice was not premature: A'zam, on his return, found his whole camp on the point of breaking up, and his women weeping and lamenting his supposed fate. Whether he felt grateful for his easy dismission does not appear; but it is recorded that he never after received a letter from his father without turning pale[1].'

One son after another was tried and found wanting by his jealous father. Mu'azzam after his seven years' captivity was sent away to govern the distant province of Kábul. A'zam, who had shown considerable zeal in the Deccan wars, was dismissed to the government of Gújarát. Aurangzíb, though painfully conciliatory to these two sons, and lavish of presents and kind words, seems never to have won their love. At one time he showed a preference for Prince Akbar, whose insurrection among the Rájputs soured his fatherly affection and increased his dread of his sons' ambition. Towards the close of his life he was drawn closer to his youngest son, Kám-Bakhsh,

[1] Elphinstone (1866), pp. 667, 668.

whose mother, Udaipúrí Bái, was the only woman for whom the Emperor entertained anything approaching to passionate love[1]. The young Prince was suspected of trafficking the imperial honour with the Maráthás, and placed under temporary arrest, but his father forgave or acquitted him, and his last letters breathe a tone of tender affection which contradicts the tenour of his domestic life.

His officers were treated with the same consideration, and the same distrust, as his elder sons. To judge from his correspondence, there never were generals more highly thought of by their sovereign. 'He condoles with their loss of relations, inquires about their illnesses, confers honours in a flattering manner, makes his presents more acceptable by the gracious way in which they are given, and scarcely ever passes a censure without softening it by some obliging expression:' but he keeps all the real power and patronage in his own hands, and shifts his governors from place to place, and surrounds them with spies, lest they should acquire undue local influence. It would be a gross injustice to ascribe his universal graciousness to calculating diplomacy, though his general leniency and dislike to severe punishments,

[1] Aurangzíb's wives played but a small part in his life. According to Manucci the chief wife was a Rájput princess, and became the mother of Muhammad and Mu'azzam, besides a daughter. A Persian lady was the mother of A'zam and Akbar and two daughters. The nationality of the third, by whom the Emperor had one daughter, is not recorded. Udaipúrí, the mother of Kám-Bakhsh, was a Christian from Georgia, and had been purchased by Dárá, on whose execution she passed to the harím of Aurangzíb.

savė when his religion or his throne was at stake, were no doubt partly due to a politic desire to avoid making needless enemies. Aurangzíb was naturally clement, just, and benevolent: but all his really kind actions were marred by the taint of suspicion, and lacked the quickening touch of trusting love. He never made a friend.

The end of the lonely unloved life was approaching. Failure stamped every effort of the final years. The Emperor's long absence had given the rein to disorders in the north; the Rájputs were in open rebellion, the Játs had risen about Agra, and the Sikhs began to make their name notorious in Multán. The Deccan was a desert, where the track of the Maráthás was traced by pillaged towns, ravaged fields, and smoking villages. The Mughal army was enfeebled and demoralized, 'those infernal foot-soldiers' were croaking like rooks in an invaded rookery, clamouring for their arrears of pay. The finances were in hopeless confusion, and Aurangzíb refused to be pestered about them. The Maráthás became so bold that they plundered on the skirts of the Grand Army, and openly scoffed at the Emperor, and no man dared leave the Mughal lines without a strong escort. There was even a talk of making terms with the insolent bandits.

At last the Emperor led the dejected remnant of his once powerful army, in confusion and alarm, pursued by skirmishing bodies of exultant Maráthás, back to Ahmadnagar, whence, more than twenty years before, he had set out full of sanguine hope, and at the head of a splendid and invincible host. His long privations had at length told upon his health, and when he entered the city he said that his journeys were over. Even when convinced that the end was near, his invincible suspicions still mastered his natural affections. He kept all his sons away, lest they should do even as he had done to his own father. Alone he had lived, and alone he made ready to die. He had all the Puritan's sense of sin and unworthiness, and his morbid creed inspired a terrible dread of death. He poured out his troubled heart to his sons in letters which show the love which all his suspicion could not uproot.

'Peace be with you and yours,' he wrote to Prince A'zam, 'I am grown very old and weak, and my limbs are feeble. Many were around me when I was born, but now I am going alone. I know not why I am or wherefore I came into the world. I bewail the moments which I have spent forgetful of God's worship. I have not done well by the country or its people. My years have gone by profitless. God has been in my heart, yet my darkened eyes have not recognized his light. Life is transient, and the lost moment never comes back. There is no hope for me in the future. The fever is gone: but only skin and dried flesh are mine. . . . The army is confounded and without heart or help, even as I am: apart from God, with no rest for the heart. They know not whether they have a King or not. Nothing brought I into this world, but I carry away with me the burthen of my sins. I know not what punishment be in store for me to suffer. Though my trust is in the mercy and goodness of God, I deplore my sins. When I have lost hope in myself, how can I hope in others? Come what will, I have launched my bark upon the waters. . . . Farewell! Farewell! Farewell!'

To his favourite Kám-Bakhsh he wrote:—

'Soul of my soul . . . Now I am going alone. I grieve for your helplessness. But what is the use? Every torment I have inflicted, every sin I have committed, every wrong I have done, I carry the consequences with me. Strange that I came with nothing into the world, and now go away with this stupendous caravan of sin! . . . Wherever I look I see only God. . . . I have greatly sinned, and I know not what torment awaits me. . . . Let not Muslims be slain and the reproach fall upon my useless head. I commit you and your sons to God's care, and bid you farewell. I am sorely troubled. Your sick mother, Udaipúrí, would fain die with me . . . Peace!'

On Friday, the 4th of March, 1707, in the fiftieth year of his reign, and the eighty-ninth of his life, after performing the morning prayers and repeating the creed, the Emperor Aurangzíb gave up the ghost. In accordance with his command, 'Carry this creature of dust to the nearest burial-place, and lay him in the earth with no useless coffin,' he was buried simply near Daulatábád beside the tombs of Muslim saints.

'Every plan that he formed came to little good; every enterprise failed:' such is the comment of the Muhammadan historian on the career of the sovereign whom he justly extols for his 'devotion, austerity, and justice,' and his 'incomparable courage, long-suffering, and judgment.' Aurangzíb's life had been a vast failure, indeed, but he had failed grandly. He had pitted his conscience against the world, and the world had triumphed over it. He had marked out a path of duty and had steadfastly pursued it, in spite of its utter impracticability. The man of the world smiles at his shortsighted policy, his ascetic ideal, his zeal for the truth as he saw it. Aurangzíb would have found his way smooth and strewn with roses had he been able to become a man of the world. His glory is that he could not force his soul, that he dared not desert the colours of his faith. He lived and died in leading a forlorn hope, and if ever the cross of heroic devotion to a lost cause belonged to mortal man, it was his. The great Puritan of India was of such stuff as wins the martyr's crown.

His glory is for himself alone. The triumph of character ennobled only himself. To his great empire his devoted zeal was an unmitigated curse. In his last letters he besought his sons not to strive against each other. Yet 'I foresee,' he wrote, 'that there will be much bloodshed. May God, the Ruler of hearts, implant in yours the will to succour your subjects, and give you wisdom in the governance of the people.' His foresight presaged something of the evil that was to come, the fratricidal struggle, the sufferings of the people. But the reality was worse than his worst fears. It was happy for him that a veil concealed from his dying eyes the shame and ignominy of the long line of impotent successors that desecrated his throne, the swelling tide of barbarous invaders from the south, the ravages of Persian and Afghán armies from the north, and the final triumph of the infidel traders upon whose small beginnings in the east and west of his wide dominions he had hardly condescended to bestow a glance. When Lord Lake entered Delhi in 1803, he was shown a miserable blind old imbecile, sitting under a tattered canopy. It was Sháh-'Álam, 'King of the World,' but captive of the Maráthás, a wretched travesty of the Emperor of India. The British General gravely saluted the shadow of the Great Mogul. To such a pass had the empire of Akbar been brought by the fatal conscience of Aurangzíb. The *ludibrium rerum humanarum* was never more pathetically played. No curtain ever dropped on a more woeful tragedy.

Yet Akbar's Dream has not wholly failed of its fulfilment. The heroic bigotry of Aurangzíb might indeed for a while destroy those bright hopes of tolerant wisdom, but the ruin was not for ever. In the progress of the ages the 'vision glorious' has found its accomplishment, and the desire of the great Emperor has been attained. Let Akbar speak in the latest words of our own lost Poet:—

> 'Me too the black-winged Azrael overcame,
> But Death hath ears and eyes; I watched my son,
> And those that follow'd, loosen, stone from stone,
> All my fair work; and from the ruin arose
> The shriek and curse of trampled millions, even
> As in the time before; but while I groan'd,
> From out the sunset pour'd an alien race,
> Who fitted stone to stone again, and Truth,
> Peace, Love and Justice came and dwelt therein.'

INDEX.

RULERS OF INDIA:

THE CLARENDON PRESS SERIES OF INDIAN HISTORICAL RETROSPECTS.

Edited by Sir W. W. Hunter, K.C.S.I., C.I.E.

Price 2s. 6d. each.

The following volumes have been arranged for up to March, 1893:—

I. *AKBAR: and the Rise of the Mughal Empire*, by Colonel Malleson, C.S.I., Author of *A History of the Indian Mutiny; The History of Afghanistan; Herat, &c.* [Published.] Third thousand.

II. *ALBUQUERQUE: and the Early Portuguese Settlements in India*, by H. Morse Stephens, Esq., Balliol College, Lecturer on Indian History at Cambridge, Author of *The French Revolution; The Story of Portugal, &c.* [Published.]

III. *AURANGZÍB: and the Decay of the Mughal Empire*, by Stanley Lane Poole, Esq., B.A., Author of *The Coins of the Mughal Emperors; The Life of Stratford Canning; Catalogue of Indian Coins in the British Museum, &c.* [Published.]

IV. *MADHAVA RAO SINDHIA: and the Hindú Reconquest of India*, by H. G. Keene, Esq., M.A., C.I.E., Author of *The Moghul Empire, &c.* [Published.]

V. *LORD CLIVE: and the Establishment of the English in India*, by Colonel Malleson, C.S.I. [In the Press.]

VI. *DUPLEIX: and the Struggle for India by the European Nations*, by Colonel Malleson, C.S.I., Author of *The History of the French in India, &c.* [Published.]

VII. *WARREN HASTINGS: and the Founding of the British Administration*, by Captain L. J. Trotter, Author of *India under Victoria, &c.* [Published.] Third thousand.

VIII. *THE MARQUESS CORNWALLIS: and the Consolidation of British Rule*, by W. S. Seton-Karr, Esq., sometime Foreign Secretary to the Government of India, Author of *Selections from the Calcutta Gazettes*, 3 vols. (1784–1805). [Published.]

IX. *THE MARQUESS WELLESLEY: and the Development of the Company into the Supreme Power in India*, by the Rev. W. H. Hutton, M.A., Fellow of St. John's College, Oxford. [In the Press.]

X. *THE MARQUESS OF HASTINGS: and the Final Overthrow of the Maráthá Power*, by Major Ross of Bladensburg, C.B., Coldstream Guards; F.R.G.S. [Published.]

XI. *MOUNTSTUART ELPHINSTONE: and the Making of South-Western India*, by J. S. Cotton, Esq., M.A., formerly Fellow of Queen's College, Oxford, Author of *The Decennial Statement of the Moral and Material Progress and Condition of India*, presented to Parliament (1885), &c. [Published.]

XII. *SIR THOMAS MUNRO: and the British Settlement of the Madras Presidency*, by John Bradshaw, Esq., M.A., LL.D., H.M.'s Inspector of Schools, Madras. [In the Press.]

XIII. *EARL AMHERST: and the British Advance eastwards to Burma*, chiefly from unpublished papers of the Auckland family, by T. W. Richmond Ritchie, Esq., of the India Office.

Works by Stanley Lane-Poole.

Stories from the Arabian Nights. 16mo. 3 vols. pp. vii, 338, 331, 346. Six Illustrations. Putnam. 1891.

The History of the Moghul Emperors illustrated by their Coins. pp. clxxvii. Constable. 1892.

Cairo: Sketches of its History, Monuments, and Social Life. Numerous Illustrations. 8vo, pp. xiv, 320. Virtue. 1892.

Aurangzíb. Rulers of India Series. 8vo, pp. 212. Clarendon Press. 1893.

Lane's Arabic-English Lexicon. Vols. 6-8. Imp. 4to, pp. xxxix, 2221-3064. Edited. Williams and Norgate. 1877-1893.

NUMISMATIC WORKS.

Catalogue of the Collection of Oriental Coins belonging to Colonel C. Seton Guthrie, R.E. Fasc. I. pp. viii, 38. Five Autotype Plates. (Also Large-Paper Edition.) Austin. 1874.

International Numismata Orientalia. Part II.—Coins of the Turkumans. 4to, pp. xii, 44. Six Plates. Trübner. 1875.

Essays in Oriental Numismatics. First, Second, and Third Series. Plates. 8vo. 3 vols. 1874, 1877, 1892.

Catalogue of Oriental Coins in the British Museum. Printed by order of the Trustees. 8vo. 10 vols. (Ouvrage couronné par l'Institut de France, 1881.)

Vol. I. THE KHALIFS. pp. xx, 263. Eight Autotype Plates. 1875.
II. MOHAMMADAN DYNASTIES. pp. xii, 279. Eight Autotype Plates. 1876.
III. THE TURKUMANS. pp. xxvi, 305. Twelve Autotype Plates. 1877.
IV. EGYPT. pp. xxx, 279. Eight Autotype Plates. 1879.
V. The MOORS and ARABIA. pp. lii, 175. Seven Autotype Plates. 1808.
VI. The MONGOLS. pp. lxxv, 300. Nine Autotype Plates. 1881.
VII. BUKHARA. pp. xlviii, 131. Five Autotype Plates. 1882.
VIII. The TURKS. pp. li, 431. Twelve Autotype Plates. 1883.
IX. X. ADDITIONS: 1875—1889. 2 vols. pp. 420, 460. Twenty Autotype Plates, and General Index. 1889, 1890.

Catalogue of Indian Coins in the British Museum. Printed by order of the Trustees. 8vo. 3 vols.

Vol. I. SULTANS of DEHLI. pp. xiv, 199. Nine Autotype Plates. 1884.
II. MOHAMMADAN STATES. pp. lxxx, 239. Twelve Autotype Plates. 1885.
III. MOGHUL EMPERORS. pp. cliii, 401. Thirty-three Autotype Plates. 1892.

Catalogue of Arabic Glass Weights in the British Museum. 8vo, pp. xxxv, 127. Nine Autotype Plates. Printed by order of the Trustees. 1891.

Coins and Medals: their Place in History and Art. By the Authors of the British Museum Official Catalogues. Edited. Illustrated. 8vo, pp. x, 286. Elliot Stock, 1885. *Second Edition.* 1892.

Catalogue of the Mohammadan Coins in the Bodleian Library, Oxford. pp. xvi, 55. Four Plates. Clarendon Press. 1888.

The Cabinet of Oriental Coins at Christ Church, Oxford. 8vo, pp. 8. Virtue. 1886.

THE END.